KNOWING JESUS

Being on the Right Side of History

Kenneth Myers

ISBN 979-8-89428-628-0 (paperback)
ISBN 979-8-89428-629-7 (digital)

Christian Faith Publishing
832 Park Avenue
Meadville, PA 16335
www.christianfaithpublishing.com

Printed in the United States of America

Contents

Introduction

It is better to trust in the Lord than to put confidence in princes.

—Psalm 118:9

Recently, several societal influencers have told us that we need to be found on the right side of history, implying that our cultural mores need to be abandoned, and the basis of our society needs to be rethought. Since Western civilization is based on Jewish Christian principles, I thought that it would be wise for us to determine just who Jesus Christ is and to see what he has to say about the future history of mankind. In this work, we set out to determine who Jesus is. We will do this by using the recorded words of the Old Testament prophets and Jesus's own words as found in the Christian New Testament of the Bible. As we seek to know Jesus more fully, we start our inquiry in the book of Malachi chapter 3, verse 1.

Postscript: Moving forward, we will (with the help of the Holy Spirit) place scripture upon scripture and build our understanding piece by piece until we come into a fuller understanding of who Jesus is. This methodology is described in Isaiah chapter 28, verses 9 and 10, and reads, **"To whom shall he teach knowledge? To them that are weaned from the milk. For precept must be upon precept, line upon line, here a little, and there a little."**

CHAPTER 1

Malachi 3:1

Behold, I will send <u>my messenger</u>, and he shall prepare the way before me: and the Lord (113—Adon), whom you seek, will suddenly come to his temple, even <u>the messenger of the covenant</u>, whom you delight in: Behold, he shall come, saith the Lord of hosts.

—Yehovah Tsaba

Looking into Malachi 3:1, we see that the Lord of hosts is telling us what he will do. He will send his messenger to prepare the way before him. Who is this messenger (messenger no. 1)?

Matthew 11:9–11 identifies John the Baptist as the first messenger, with Jesus saying, "What did you go out into the wilderness to see? A prophet? Yes, more than a prophet. For this is he, of whom it is written, 'Behold, I send my messenger before thy face, which shall prepare the way before thee.'"

And the Adon (sovereign Lord) whom you (Israel) seek will suddenly come to his temple. Who is the Adon? We find the title Adon in Psalm 110:1, which reads, "Yehovah said to my Adon, 'Sit at my right hand, until I make your enemies your footstool.'" To this scripture, Jesus makes reference in Matthew 22:41–45: And when the Pharisees were gathered together, Jesus asked them a series of two questions: (1) "What think ye of the Christ? Whose son is he?" and (2) "If David calls him Lord, how can he be his son?"

We also see that the Adon will come suddenly to his temple. Many may believe that the Lord of hosts was referring to the temple in Jerusalem, but he was actually speaking of his body.

In John 2:19–22, Jesus tells us that his body is that temple when he said, "Destroy this temple, and in three days I will raise it up." (Now this he spoke of the temple of his body. And when he was raised from the dead, his disciples remembered that he had said this.)

Next, we see that the Adon is also identified as a messenger (messenger no. 2), a messenger of the covenant.

Luke 22:20—in this portion of Scripture, Jesus speaks of a new covenant, saying, "This cup is the new covenant (testament) in my blood, which is shed for you." Notice also that the prophet Jeremiah spoke of a coming new covenant in Jeremiah 31:31, writing, "Behold, the days are coming, says the Lord, when I will make a new covenant with the house of Israel and the house of Judah."

Connecting the dots:

This portion of Scripture found in Malachi 3:1 tells us that the Lord of hosts will send John the Baptist to go before him (i.e., before his face). And then the Son of David (i.e., the Adon spoken of in Psalm 110) will come in the flesh and be a messenger of a (new) covenant. Notice that the messenger (John the Baptist) was to go before the Lord of hosts to prepare the way for him. Jesus acknowledges that John the Baptist was sent to go before him in order to prepare the way for him. Can we infer from Malachi 3:1 that Jesus is the Lord of hosts? I think we can, and we will explore this possibility using other scriptures in chapter 2.

Next: "Revelation 1:1"

CHAPTER 2

Revelation 1:1

Revelation 1:1 reads, **"The revelation (602—*apokalupsis*) of Jesus Christ, which God gave to him, to show his servants things which must quickly come into being."**

The book of Revelation is an *apokalupsis* that is an uncovering of, or a revealing of, who Jesus is! In Revelation 1:17–18, Jesus reveals this about himself saying, **"I am the first and the last: I am he that lives, and was dead; and, behold, I am alive for evermore, and I have the keys of death and hades."**

Again, in Revelation 2:8, Jesus takes up the phrase/term "the first and the last," saying to the church in Smyrna, **"These things saith the first and the last."** I find the usage of this term very interesting, for it is also found in several prophecies in the book of Isaiah, where the Lord of hosts applies it to himself. Most telling is Isaiah 44:6, which reads, **"Thus saith the Lord, the King of Israel, and his redeemer, the Lord of hosts: I am the first, and I am the last; and beside me there is no God."**

Connecting the dots:

Jesus tells us that he is the first and the last. In Isaiah 44:6, the Lord of hosts also tells us that he is the first and the last. Therefore, by referencing Isaiah 42:8, we can conclude that Jesus must be the Lord of hosts, for it is written, "My glory will I not give to another."

Note also, according to Isaiah 44:6, if Jesus is the Lord of hosts, he is also the Lord (Yehovah) and the King of Israel. We will explore these titles in subsequent chapters, but next, we will answer the question, **"Who are you?"** as raised by the Pharisees in John 8:25.

Author's comment:

The title "Lord of hosts" in Hebrew is "Yehovah Tsaba." Yehovah is the name "I am," showing God's self-existent nature. The Hebrew word *Tsaba* comes from the word *saba*, meaning army or host. The Lord of hosts is in command of the angel army of heaven. The Lord of hosts is also frequently called upon and cited by the prophets of God as they prophesied, saying, "Thus saith the Lord of hosts." Here are just a few scriptures that mention/reference the Lord of hosts:

> But I (David) come to you (Goliath) in the
> name of the Lord of hosts. (1 Sam. 17:45)

> And Elijah said, As the Lord of hosts lives,
> before whom I stand. (1 Kings 18:15)

> And Elisha said, As the Lord of hosts lives,
> before whom I stand. (2 Kings 3:14)

> The Lord of hosts is with us; the God of
> Jacob is our refuge. (Ps. 46:7)

Next: "Who Are You?"

CHAPTER 3

Who Are You?

An interesting dialogue between Jesus and the Pharisees is recorded in John 8:23–25 and reads this way:

Jesus: You are from beneath. I am from above. You are of this world. I am not of this world. Therefore, I said unto you that you shall die in your sins, for <u>if you believe not that I am he,</u> **(1)** you shall die in your sins.

Pharisees: Who are you?

Jesus: Even the same that I said unto you <u>from the beginning</u>. **(2)**

(1) In Deuteronomy 18:18–19, Moses wrote, "I (Yehovah) will raise up a prophet from among them (the Jewish people), and I will put my words in his mouth; <u>and he shall speak unto them all that I shall command him</u>. And it shall come to pass, that whosoever will not hearken unto my words which he shall speak in my name, I will require it of him."

In this regard and for this reason, in John 12:48–50, Jesus said this: "He that rejects me, and receives not my words, has one that judges him: the word that I have spoken, the same shall judge him in the last day. For <u>I have not spoken of myself</u>; but the Father which sent me, he gave me a commandment, what I should say, and what I should speak. And I know that his commandment is life everlasting: whatsoever I speak therefore, even as the Father said to me, so I speak."

(2) "Even what I said to you from the beginning" (John 8:25)!

I believe that the use of the word *beginning* as used here by Jesus is significant because it takes our minds immediately to the very first verse of the Hebrew Bible [Genesis 1:1], which reads: "In the beginning God (430—*Elohiym*) created the heaven and the earth." Moreover, to a learned religious leader or theologian, it can also take one to Isaiah 48:12–16, which reads, "Hearken unto me, O Jacob and Israel, my called; I am he; I am the first, I also am the last. My hand has laid the foundation of the earth, and the palm of my right hand has spread out the heavens: When I call unto them, they stand up together. Come near to me, and hear this; I have not spoken in secret **(a)** from the beginning; from the time that it was, there am I: And now the Lord God [John 8:54], and his Spirit has sent me **(b)**."

Connecting the dots:

1. Moses spoke of a Prophet who would speak all that God commanded him (Deut. 18:18). Jesus stated that he had not spoken of himself (John 12:49).
2. The Father, Son, and Holy Spirit are clearly spoken of in Isaiah 48:16 and in 1 John 5:7.
3. Jesus stated that he was sent by the Father to earth (John 12:49; Isa. 48:16).
4. Jesus was there in the beginning of creation (Isa. 48:16; John 1:1–3; Mic. 5:2).

Addendum:

(a) In John 18:20, Jesus told Caiaphas, the high priest, that he had spoken openly to the world, and he spoke nothing in secret. Regarding his teachings, Jesus said, "Ask those who heard me. They know what I said."

(b) Jesus said in John 8:42, "I proceeded forth and came from God (My Father). I came not of my own self, but he sent me."

Lastly, at this time, we must point out that the one that the Jewish people spoke of as their God, is the one that Jesus refers to as his Father (John 8:54).

Next: "The Word of God"

CHAPTER 4

The Word of God

In Genesis chapter 15, verse 1, the Word of the Lord came to Abraham in a vision, saying, "Fear not, Abram; I am thy shield, and your exceeding great reward." As we see in verse 2, Abraham spoke to the Word of the Lord, addressing him as the Lord God. In Genesis chapter 15, the Word of the Lord comes to Abraham, and it is not just a spoken prophetic word but consists of a visual being, who speaks and interacts with Abraham. This is the first time in the Bible where the term "Word of" is found in the scriptures.

Unquestionably, the most prominent use of the title "Word of God" occurs in John 1:1–3. This portion of Scripture speaks of Jesus Christ as the Word of God. This portion of Scripture tells us that from the beginning of time, Jesus was with God and was God and that all things came into being through him. The first-century church fathers taught that all things were made through Jesus Christ. The book of Hebrews states that God (the Father) made the ages through his Son (Heb. 1:2). Similarly, the apostle Paul wrote the following in his letter to the Colossians (Col. 1:15–17), saying: "He (Jesus) is the image of the invisible God, the firstborn of every creature (2937 *ktisis*—formation): For in him were all things created (2936 *ktizo*—founded), the things in heaven and the things on earth, the visible and the invisible, whether thrones, or dominions, or principalities, or powers: all things were created (2936—founded) through him and for him: He is before all things, and in him all things consist (hold together)." In Paul's epistle to the Ephesians, we are told that in the future, God (the Father) plans to gather together all things in heaven and on earth and place them under the administration of his Son, Jesus Christ (Eph. 1:10).

Revelation 19:13–14 tells us that Jesus Christ is the Word of God. He is King of kings and Lord of lords, and the armies of heaven follow him into battle. The apostle Paul told Timothy (1 Tim. 6:15–16) that in his time, Jesus Christ will prove who is the only potentate, the King of kings, and the Lord of lords, for only Jesus holds the key to immortality (Rev. 1:18), and he alone dwells in the unapproachable light, which no man has seen or can see.

It should also be noted at this time that our discussion of the Word of God introduces us to the concept of the Trinity. Simply put, as Christians, we believe that there is one God who manifests himself as the Father, as the Son, and as the Holy Spirit. This relationship within the Godhead is stated in 1 John 5:7 and also seen in Isaiah 48:16. John 1:18 tells us that no man (nothing) can see God (the Father) and that the Father reveals himself to his creation through his Son.

Review of the above-cited scriptures:

> The word of the Lord (Yehovah) came to Abram in a vision, saying, Fear not, Abram: I am thy shield, and your exceeding great reward. (Gen. 15:1)

> In the beginning was the Word, and the Word was with God, and the Word was God. The same was in the beginning with God. All things were made through him; and without him was not anything made that was made. (John 1:1–3)

God has in these last days spoken unto us in his Son, whom he has appointed heir of all things, by whom also he made the worlds. (Heb. 1:2)

He (Jesus) is the image of the invisible God, the first product of every formation: For in him were all things founded, that which is in heaven, and that which is on the earth, whether they be thrones, or dominions, or principalities, or powers: all things were founded through him, and for him: And he is before all things, and in him all things hold together. (Col. 1:15–17)

That in the administration of the fullness of times he (God the Father) might gather together in one all things in Christ, both which are in heaven, and which are on earth. (Eph. 1:10)

And he (Jesus) was clothed with a vesture dipped in blood: and his name is called The Word of God. And the armies which were in heaven followed him upon white horses, clothed in fine linen, white and clean. And he has on his vesture and on his thigh a name written, KING OF KINGS AND LORD OF LORDS. (Rev. 19:13–16)

Who in his times he shall show, who is the blessed and only Potentate, the King of Kings, and the Lord of lords; the only one holding immortality, dwelling in unapproachable light, that which no man has seen, nor can see. (1 Tim. 6:15–16)

I (Jesus) am he that lives, I was dead; and, behold, I am alive for evermore, and I hold the keys of hell and of death. (Rev. 1:18)

For there are three that bear record in heaven, the Father, the Word, and the Holy Spirit: and these three are one. (1 John 5:7)

Come near to me, and hear this; I have not spoken in secret from the beginning; from the time that it was, there am I: And now the Lord God, and his Spirit has sent me. (Isa. 48:16)

Nothing (3762 *oudeis*—not even one thing) has ever seen God, the only begotten Son in the Father's bosom reveals (1834—unfolds, explains) him. (John 1:18)

Connecting the dots:

1. Genesis 15:1 shows us that the Word of God is a walking, talking person, someone that can be seen and heard.
2. First John 5:7 speaks of a Godhead, a Trinity made of three persons.
3. Isaiah 48:16 (chapter 3) also speaks of such a Trinity.
4. Jesus is the Word of God (Rev. 19:13).
5. Jesus is the firstborn of every formation (Col. 1:15).
6. Jesus is the King of kings and the Lord of lords (Rev. 19:16; 1 Tim. 6:15).
7. He was with God (the Father) (John 17:5; Isa. 48:16).
8. Jesus is God in the flesh (John 1:14; Isa. 44:6; John 5:23).
9. Everything that exists came into being through Jesus (John 1:1–3).
10. All things were created through Jesus and for him (Col. 1:16; Rev. 4:11).
11. Jesus and the Father are one (John 10:30).

Final thought: Who has believed our report? (Isa. 53:1)

> And <u>the Word</u> became flesh, and lived among us. (John 1:14)

> That which was from the beginning, which we (apostles) have heard, which we have seen with our eyes, which we have looked upon, and our hands have handled, of <u>the Word</u> of life; for the life was manifested, and we have seen it, and bear witness, and show unto you that eternal life, which was with the Father, and was manifested to us. That which we have seen and heard declare we unto you. (1 John 1:1–3)

Author's note: The apostle John and the other apostles saw both the human mortal existence of Jesus (John 1:14) and the after-resurrection, glorified, immortal existence of Jesus (1 John 1:1–3). While their first exposure was instructional and challenging to their belief system, the second exposure was incomprehensible, causing the apostle Thomas to cry out, "My Lord and my God" (John 20:28) Now, you may ask, "What do we have here?" Here we see the firstborn of a new creation originating out of Adam's race (Col. 1:15), a prototype, the firstborn among many brethren (Rom. 8:29).

> And so, to as many as received him (Jesus), to them gave he the authority to become the sons of God, even to them that believed into his name. (John 1:12; Eph. 1:5)

Next: "The Kenosis"

CHAPTER 5

The Kenosis

And the Word became flesh and lived among us.

—John 1:14

The kenosis is the theological term used in connection with the incarnation of Jesus Christ. It is derived from the Greek word *kenoo* (2758), which means to make empty. Simply stated, the doctrine is this: God laid down his nature and took on our human nature. He was born of a woman and therefore became a member of Adam's progeny, and as such, he is a Son of Adam (i.e., Son of Man). This teaching is found in Philippians chapter 2, verses 5 through 8, and reads as follows:

Let this mind be in you, which was also in Christ Jesus: for although he was in the form (3444 *morphe*) of God...he emptied (2758 *kenoo*) himself, taking on the form (3444) of a slave, becoming in the likeness of men: And in fashion being found as a man, he humbled him-

self, and became obedient unto death, even the
death of the cross.

In this respect Jesus taught the following:

1. That he was from above, that he was not of this world
    (John 8:23).
2. That the Father sent him (John 7:29).
3. That he laid down his life of his own accord (John 10:18).
4. That he came from the Father and that he was going to
    leave the world and return to the Father (John 16:28).

Moreover, because of this, Jesus made these statements:

> No man has ascended up to heaven, but he
> that came down from heaven, even the <u>Son of
> man</u> which is in heaven. (John 3:13)

> What would you think if you saw the <u>Son
> of man</u> ascend up to where he was before? (John
> 6:62)

> Before Abraham was I am. (John 8:58)

The prophet Micah touched upon this subject when he foretold
of Jesus's birth, saying, **"And you, Bethlehem Ephratah, though
you be little among the thousands of Judah, yet out of you shall
he come forth unto me that is to be ruler in Israel; whose goings
forth have been of old, <u>from everlasting</u>" (Mic. 5:2).**
In the Gospel of Luke, we are told that the birth of Jesus Christ
came into being when the Holy Spirit came upon Mary. The angel
Gabriel foretold of his birth, stating that the baby was to be called
Jesus and that he would be called the Son of God and that he would
reign over the house of Jacob forever (Luke 1:30–35). This is in
agreement with the prophecy recorded in Isaiah 7:14, which states,

"Behold, a virgin shall conceive and bear a son, and call his name Immanuel, which means God with us."

Isaiah 9:6–7 tells us that a son shall be born in Israel and that the government shall be upon his shoulders, and his name shall be called wonderful, counsellor, the mighty God, the everlasting Father, the Prince of peace. The increase of his government and its peace shall know no end, and he shall sit upon the throne of David, for the Lord of hosts will perform this (Isa. 9:6–7).

The apostle Paul puts it this way:

> When the time was right, God sent forth his Son, made of a woman, made under the law, to redeem them that were under the law, that we might be adopted as sons of God. (Gal. 4:4–5; Eph. 1:5)

Similarly, Hebrews chapter 2, verses 14 and 16 tells us this:

> For as much then as the children (of Adam) are partakers of flesh and blood, he (Jesus) also himself likewise took part of the same; that through death he might destroy him (the devil) that had the power of death. For he (Jesus) took not on him the nature of angels; but he took on him the seed of Abraham.

This was necessary because in Adam all died, but in Christ shall all be made alive (1 Cor. 15:22). Therefore, Jesus proclaimed, "I am the resurrection and the life: he that believes in me, though he die, yet shall he live." And I, said Jesus, "Have the keys of hades and of death" (Rev. 1:18; 1 Tim. 6:16).

Connecting the dots:

1. Jesus existed in heaven before he was born on earth.
2. He took on our human nature and therefore can refer to himself as the Son of Man.
3. He is God in the flesh.
4. Only Jesus has power over death; he holds the key to eternal life.

Next: "I Am in the Father, and the Father Is in Me"

I Am in the Father, and the Father Is in Me

In 2 Corinthians chapter 5, verse 19, the apostle Paul tells us that God was in Christ, reconciling the world to himself.

Jesus said the following:

> If I honor myself, my honor is nothing: it is my Father that honors me; of whom you say, that he is your God. (John 8:54)

> Say ye of him, whom the Father has sanctified, and sent into the world, You blaspheme; because I said, I am the Son of God.* If I do not the works of my Father, believe me not. But if I

---

* Therefore the Jewish leaders sought to kill Jesus, because he not only broke the rules of the sabbath, but he also said that God was his Father, <u>making himself equal with God</u> (John 5:18).

do, though you believe me not, believe the works: that you may know, and believe, that the Father is in me, and I in him. (John 10:36–38)

Do you not believe that I am in the Father, and the Father in me? The words that I speak to you I speak not of myself; but the Father that dwells in me, he does the works. Believe me: I am in the Father, and the Father in me; or else believe me for the very works' sake. (John 14:10–11)

If you had known me, you would have known my Father also:† and from henceforth you know him, and have seen him…for he that has seen me has seen the Father.‡ (John 14:7–9)

Great is the mystery of godliness: God was manifest in the flesh, justified in the Spirit, seen of angels, preached to the Gentiles, believed on in the world, received up into glory. (1 Tim. 3:16)

Connecting the dots:

- Doubting Thomas had it right when he exclaimed, "My Lord and my God" (John 20:28).
- Jesus Christ was/is God in the flesh (Isa. 7:14; John 1:14).

Next: "The Messiah"

---

† Nothing has seen God (the Father) at any time; the only begotten Son, which is in the bosom of the Father, he has declared him (John 1:18).

‡ Jesus is the image of the invisible God, the firstborn of every formation (Col. 1:15; Heb. 1:3).

CHAPTER 7

The Messiah

The word *messiah* contains the idea of being anointed. The Messiah is the anointed one of God. God has anointed him to be King. He will be a righteous and equitable King, and his kingdom will be one of peace and prosperity. The kingdom that the Messiah rules over is one that cannot be destroyed and is therefore an everlasting kingdom. It must be noted that the title "Christ" is the Greek equivalent of the Hebrew title Messiah. (This equivalency can be seen in John 1:41 and John 4:25.)

In John 1:41, Andrew told his brother Simon that he had found the Messiah/Christ, referring to Jesus of Nazareth.

And John 4:25–26 records a conversation that Jesus had with a woman at Jacob's well. In this discussion, the woman stated that she awaited the coming of the Messiah, the one they called the Christ, to which Jesus replied, "I that speak to you am he."

In Matthew chapter 16, verses 13 through 17, Jesus asked his disciples, "Who do the people say that I am?"

They replied, "Some say you are Elijah or Jeremiah or one of the other prophets." Then Jesus asked them, "But who do you say that I am?"

"You are the Christ (the Messiah), the Son of the living God," replied Simon Peter.

Jesus responded, "Flesh and blood has not revealed this to you but my Father, which is in heaven, and it is upon this rock that I will build my church."

In Mark chapter 14, we see the preliminary trial occurring before the chief priests and council as they attempted to develop charges against Jesus that could be presented to Pilate. When all the attempts failed to obtain the necessary condemning evidence against Jesus, the high priest asked him (Mark 14:61–62), "Are you the Christ, the Son of the Blessed?"

Jesus answered, "I am," and so they presented him to Pilate, saying, "We have a law, and under that law this man ought to die, because he made himself the Son of God" (John 19:7).

<u>Connecting the dots:</u>

- Jesus confessed to be the Messiah.
- Jesus was crucified because he claimed to be the Messiah (i.e., the Christ, the Son of the Blessed).
- Jesus did not openly teach that he was the Messiah because the time for his messianic kingdom had not fully come (i.e., it was to be a future event) (Matt. 16:20; John 2:4; John 18:33–37; 1 Tim. 6:15).

Author's note:

Throughout history, God has used holy men and women, led by the Holy Spirit, to direct, keep, and guide mankind (Heb. 1:1; 2 Pet. 1:21). However, when it came to restoring/redeeming mankind to himself, no son of Adam was qualified to perform this task (Rom. 3:23–26; 1 John 3:5; Rev. 5:2–14). In order to satisfy his own requirements and complete the task, it was necessary for God himself to take on human nature (i.e., to become the Son of Man) (Heb. 2:14–16). Therefore, the Word of God became a man and accomplished what no man would or could do.

Next: "The Suffering Messiah"

CHAPTER 8

The Suffering Messiah

Point no. 1

The prophet Isaiah spoke of a suffering servant (Messiah) in the fifty-third chapter of the book that bears his name. Here are some of the things that Isaiah tells us about the suffering Messiah:

1. He would be rejected and despised by men (verse 3).
2. He would be wounded for our transgressions and bruised for our iniquities (verse 5).
3. He would be oppressed by men (verse 7).
4. He would be like a lamb brought to the slaughter (verse 7).
5. He would be killed for the transgressions of the people (verse 8).
6. He will make his soul a sin offering (verse 10).
7. He was numbered with the transgressors (verse 12).
8. He had done no violence (verse 9).
9. There was no deceit in him (verse 9).
10. The pleasure of the Lord shall prosper in his hands (verse 10).
11. By his knowledge, he shall justify many (verse 11).
12. He will divide the spoil with the strong (verse 12).

Point no. 2

The application of Isaiah 53 is tied to Jesus Christ of Nazareth in Acts 8:32–33, which records a discussion involving Philip, a disciple of Jesus Christ and a man of Ethiopia, who was reading chapter 53 of Isaiah.

"Who is the prophet writing about," asked the Ethiopian. "Who is the lamb, the one led to the slaughter?"

In response to his questions, Philip then began at the cited scripture (Isa. 53:7–8) to tell the man about Jesus Christ.

Point no. 3

The early church fathers taught that the Old Testament prophets had prophesied that the Christ would suffer first, and thereafter the glory of the Messiah would follow (Acts 3:18–21; Acts 26:23; 1 Pet. 1:11). We see these two phases of the Messiah being taught and explained by the apostle Peter in the third chapter of Acts.

> But those things, which God before had shown by the mouth of all his prophets, that Christ should suffer, he has so fulfilled. Repent therefore, and be converted, that your sins may be blotted out, when the times of refreshing shall come from the Lord; and he shall send Jesus Christ, which before was preached unto you: Whom the heaven must receive until the times of restitution of all things, which God has spoken by the mouth of all his holy prophets since the world began. (Acts 3:18–21; Rev. 10:7)

(Note that phase 1 involves a suffering Messiah dying for the sins of mankind, and phase 2 involves a Messiah who will reign over the earth with glory and power. Note also that there appears to be a time interval between the two phases (i.e., whom the heaven must receive until the times of restitution of all things), giving mankind the opportunity to repent and conform to God's plan of salvation).

Point no. 4

We also clearly see two distinct phases (advents) of the Messiah with a time interval separating the two phases in Micah 5:2–4 (In verse 2, we see phase 1; the king is born. In verse 3, we see the existence of a time interval, and in verse 4, we see the greatness of his reign.) In the New Testament, entry into Micah's prophecy occurs in Matthew 2:1–6, when the Magi ask King Herod, "Where is he that is <u>born King of the Jews</u>" (Matthew 2:2)? The answer provided in Matthew 2:5–6 takes us directly to the prophecy found in Micah 5:2–5, which reads as follows:

> But you Bethlehem Ephratah, though you be little among the thousands of Judah, yet out of you shall he come forth unto me that is to be ruler in Israel; whose goings forth have been of old (John 8:58), from everlasting (i.e., days of eternity).
>
> **Therefore will he give them up (Matt. 23:37–39), until the time that she which travails (Jer. 30:4–7) has brought forth (Ps. 118:18–26]: Then the remnant of his brethren shall return unto the children of Israel (Rev. 7:3–4; Ps. 110:3).**
>
> And he shall stand and feed in the strength of the Lord, in the majesty of the name of the Lord his God (John 20:17); and they (Israel) shall abide: For now shall he be great unto the ends of the earth (Jer. 23:5–8; Zeph. 3:15).
>
> And this man shall be peace.

We can also see this time interval occurring in Jesus's answer to the question, "Are you the Christ, the Son of the Blessed?" When he answered, "I am, and you shall see the Son of man sitting in the right hand of power, and coming in the clouds of heaven" (Mark 14:61–62) and, again, when Pilate asked Jesus, "Are you King of the Jews?" To which Jesus replies, "To this end was I born, and for this cause came I into the world" (John 18:33–37). Notice also that a change in an interval of time is indicated in Matthew 19:28, when Jesus said to his disciples, "Verily I say to you, that followed me: <u>in the regeneration (new beginning)</u> when the Son of man shall sit in the throne of his glory, you also shall sit upon twelve thrones, judging the twelve tribes of Israel."

"My time is not yet come," said Jesus (John 7:6, 2:4), but in his times, he shall show who is the blessed and only potentate, the King of kings, and the Lord of lords (1 Tim. 6:15).

Point no. 5

Revelation 5:1–14 also gives us a heavenly vision of the suffering Messiah, with him being presented to us in the person of a slain Lamb. Here is a brief review of Revelation 5:1–14:

1. No man is found worthy to open the scroll (Rev. 5:1–4).
2. The slain Lamb, who is the root of David, has overcome (the flesh, the world, sin, Satan, evil), and he is worthy to open the scroll (Rev. 5:5–6).
3. The Lamb takes the scroll out of the hand of him that sits upon the throne (Rev. 5:7).
4. The four zoons and the twenty-four elders fall down and worship the Lamb (Rev. 5:8–10).
5. All creation enters into the worship—worshipping the Lamb and him that sits upon the throne (i.e., him that lives forever and ever) (Rev. 5:11–14).

> And they sung a new song, saying, "You are worthy to take the scroll, and to open the seals thereof: for you were slain, <u>and have redeemed us to God by your blood</u> out of every kindred, and tongue, and people, and nation; and you have

made us unto our God kings and priests, and we
shall reign over the earth. (Rev. 5:9; Rev. 1:5–6)

Connecting the dots:

- Jesus confessed to being the Messiah (Mark 14:61–62; John 4:25–26).
- As stated in Acts 3:18–21 there are two advents (phases) associated with the prophesied Messiah. In the first advent, he appeared as the suffering Messiah, who died for the sins of mankind (John 8:24). In the second advent, he comes in glory to establish a kingdom of peace and reign over the whole earth. These two advents can also be seen in Micah 5:2–4.
- There is an interval of time between the first and second advent (the church age).
- Jesus offered himself as a sin offering (Isa. 53:10; John 10:17–18; Rev. 5:9–10).
- Jesus will come again for his kingdom (Matt. 19:28; 1 Tim. 6:15).

Next: "The King of Israel"

CHAPTER 9

The King of Israel

Point no. 1: <u>Jesus is the King of Israel.</u>

Regarding the King of Israel, **Zechariah 9:9 reads,** "Rejoice greatly, O daughter of Zion; shout, O daughter of Jerusalem: Behold, <u>your King</u> comes unto you: He is just, and having salvation; lowly, and riding upon an ass, and upon a colt the foal of an ass."

Psalm 2:6 reads, "I have set my king upon my holy hill of Zion."

John 18:37 reads, "Then Pilate said to Jesus, 'Art you a king?' And Jesus replied, 'To this end was I born, and for this cause came I into this world.' And so Pilate wrote a title which read, 'Jesus of Nazareth the King of the Jews,' and placed it upon his cross."

The prophecy presented in Zechariah 9:9 was fulfilled just several days before Christ was crucified and is commonly known and celebrated in Christian churches on Palm Sunday. The fulfillment of this prophecy occurred when Jesus was entering Jerusalem from the Mount of Olives. The events of that day are recorded in three of the four gospels, and so it is written (Matt. 21:1–11; Mark 11:1–11; Luke 19:29–44) that a great multitude of people began to rejoice and praise God with a loud voice, saying, "Hosanna to the son of

David (Matt. 21:9), blessed be <u>the King</u> that comes in the name of the Lord" (Luke 19:37–38). Several days after this event, under the authority of Pontius Pilate, Jesus was crowned with thorns and crucified. The charges written and placed on his cross read, "**This is Jesus, the King of the Jews**," thereby fulfilling the prophecy in Psalm 2:6, which reads, "I've set my King upon my holy hill of Zion."

Regarding the King of Israel, there are other Old Testament prophecies that speak of a time when the branch of David (Son of David) will peacefully reign over the earth. We find one such prophecy in Jeremiah 23:5–6, which reads, "**Behold, the days come, saith the Lord, that I will raise unto David a righteous Branch, and a King shall reign and prosper, and shall execute judgment and justice in the earth. In his days Judah shall be saved, and Israel shall dwell safely.**" Here are several other prophecies that also speak of his Messianic reign:

> And the Lord shall reign over them in mount Zion from henceforth, even forever. Unto thee shall it come, even the first dominion; the kingdom shall come to the daughter of Jerusalem. (Mic. 4:7–8)

> And they (Israel) shall abide: for now shall he be great unto the ends of the earth. (Mic. 5:4)

> And there was given to him (the Son of man) dominion, and glory, and a kingdom, that all people, nations, and languages, should serve him: His dominion is an everlasting dominion, which shall not pass away, and his kingdom that which shall not be destroyed. (Dan. 7:14)

> The Lord has taken away your judgments, he has cast out your enemy: The King of Israel, even the Lord is in the midst of thee: You shall not see evil any more. (Isa. 40:2; Zeph. 3:15)

Who (Jesus) in his times shall show, who is the blessed and only Potentate, the King of kings, and the Lord of lords. (1 Tim. 6:15; Rev. 19:11–16)

Point no. 2: <u>Jesus is the King of glory</u> because he is the Lord of hosts.

Psalm 24:1 speaks of the time in which the King of glory shall reign over all the earth (Isa. 2:2–4; 1 Tim. 6:15). It also tells us who exactly is the King of glory: The Lord, strong and mighty, the Lord, mighty in battle (Ps. 24:8; Rev. 19:11–17), is the King of glory. He is the one known as the Lord of hosts, and the Lord of hosts is the King of glory (Ps. 24:10). We have seen in our earlier chapters that Jesus is the Lord of hosts. Note also that Jesus, in John 13:13, acknowledged that he is Lord when he said, "You call me Master and Lord: and you say well; for so I am." Here is what we can learn from the twenty-fourth psalm:

> **The earth is the Lord's, and the fullness thereof; the world, and they that dwell therein. (Ps. 24:1)**

For over two thousand years, the church has been praying, "Thy kingdom come, thy will be done on earth as it is in heaven" (Matt. 6:10). In Revelation 11:15, when the seventh angel sounds his trumpet (Rev 10:7), the rapture of the church occurs (1 Cor. 15:51), and it is proclaimed in heaven that the kingdoms of this world are to become the kingdoms of our Lord and of his Christ and that he shall reign for ever and ever (Dan. 7:14). But before this occurs, something has to happen in Israel. Namely there must come forth out of Israel a generation that seeks after the God of Jacob.

> **This is the generation of them that seek him, that seek your face, O God of Jacob. (Ps. 24:6)**

In John 18:36 Jesus says, "My kingdom is not of this world, if my kingdom were of this world then would my servants fight." As stated in Isaiah 53:3, at his first coming, he was to be despised and rejected by men (John 19:15). We see this in Matthew 23:37, when Jesus laments over the city of Jerusalem, saying, "How often would I have gathered your children together, even as a hen gathers her chicks under her wings and you would not." And so, as foretold by the prophet Micah, he will give them up until the time that she, which travails, has brought forth (Jer. 30:6–7). Then the remnant of his brethren shall return unto the children of Israel (Zech. 13:8–9; Rev. 7:3–4). This turnaround is clearly indicated in Psalm 110:3, which states, "Your people shall be willing in the day of your power: In the beauties of holiness out of the womb of the new day (Acts 3:21; Matt. 19:28), you have the covering of your youth." Today, based on Psalm 24:7, we can expect to see many Jewish men and women come to Christ before the King of glory shall come to reign.

Lift up your heads, O ye gates; and be lifted up, ye everlasting doors; and the King of glory shall come in. (Ps. 24:7)

The full conversion of Israel to Jesus is found in Psalm 118 and occurs this way: Israel finds herself surrounded by enemies and fighting for her existence. Until this time, the state of Israel has put its confidence in the goodness of mankind and has trusted in the support of world rulers but has now come to discover that such hope is empty and vain. Turning to the God of Jacob is their only hope for their survival (Ps. 118:8–9; Ps. 46:11). When they call out to the Lord, God responds and comes to their aid (Rom. 11:25–26), causing Israel to proclaim this confession of faith (Ps. 118:18–29):

1. The Lord has chastened me sore (Jer. 30:7–8), but he has not given me over to death.
2. Open the gates of righteousness (John 10:7–9), and I will go in.
3. This is the gate of the Lord into which the righteous enter.

4. I will praise thee, for you have heard me, and you have become my salvation.
5. The stone, which the builders rejected, has become the chief cornerstone.
6. This is the Lord's doing; and it is marvelous in our eyes.
7. This is the day that the Lord has made (Ezek. 39:8; Rev. 16:17).
8. We beseech thee, O Lord, break forth now.
9. Blessed is he that comes in the name of the Lord (Matt. 23:39).
10. God is the Lord; he has illuminated us.
11. Thou art my God, and I will praise thee.
12. Give thanks to the Lord, for he is good, for his mercy endures forever (2 Chron. 20:21).

Who is the King of glory? The Lord strong and mighty, the Lord mighty in battle. (Ps. 24:8)

In Revelation 19:11–17, we see Jesus coming to earth to establish his kingdom. Isaiah 47:3 tells us that the returning Jesus will not be a mortal man. And Micah 7:15 tells us that his second coming will be as great or greater an event than the exodus of Moses's time. Psalm 24:10 tells us that the Lord of hosts is the King of glory. Isaiah 44:6, in conjunction with Revelation 1:17–18, tells us that Jesus is the Lord of hosts. Therefore, Jesus is the Lord of glory.

> And I (John) saw heaven open, and behold a white horse; and he that sat upon him was called The Word of God, and the armies of heaven followed him upon white horses. And out of his mouth goes a sharp sword, that with it he should smite the nations: and he shall rule them with a rod of iron (Ps. 2:9). And he has on his clothing a name written, King of kings, and Lord of lords (1 Tim. 6:15). And I saw an angel standing in

the sun; and he cried to the fowls that fly in the midst of heaven, "Come and gather yourselves together unto the supper of the great God." (Rev. 19:11–17; Ezek. 39:17–22)

I (the Lord of hosts) will take vengeance, and I will not meet you as a man. (Isa. 47:3)

According to the days of your coming out of the land of Egypt will I show unto him (the Assyrian/antichrist) marvellous things. (Mic. 7:15)

Who is this King of glory? <u>The Lord of hosts, he is the King of glory</u>. (Ps. 24:10)

Thus saith the Lord the King of Israel, and his redeemer <u>the Lord of hosts</u>; I am the first, and I am the last; and beside me there is no God. (Isa. 44:6; Rev. 1:17–18)

I (Jesus) am the first and the last: I am he that lives, I was dead; and, behold, I am alive for evermore; and I have the keys to hades and death. (Rev. 1:17–18)

<u>Connecting the dots:</u>

1. Jesus is the King of Israel.
2. Jesus is the King of glory.
3. Jesus is the Lord of hosts.

Author's comments:

Jesus is he that is and was and is to come. He is currently known as the Christ, the Messiah, the anointed of God. In ages past, he was known by various names, including Adonay, El Shadday, the

Angel of the Lord, and Lord of hosts. In the future, when he returns to establish his kingdom on earth, he will be known as the Lord of glory. Nevertheless, Jesus Christ is the same; he changes not (Mal. 3:6). He is the same yesterday, today, and forever (Heb. 13:8). Two scenes seen in heaven—Revelation 4:8–11 and Revelation 11:17–18—give credence to the fact that Jesus is he who is and was and is to come. Of particular interest is Revelation 11:17–18, which occurs immediately after the sounding of the seventh trumpet.

> And the four beasts (2226 *zoons*) say, "Holy, holy, holy, <u>Lord God Almighty</u> (Ex. 6:3), **which was, and is, and is to come**." And when those beasts (*zoons*) give glory and honor and thanks to him that sat on the throne (Rev. 3:21), <u>the one who lives for ever and ever</u> (Rev. 1:18), then the 24 elders fall down before him that sat upon the throne and worship <u>him that lives for ever and ever</u> saying, "Thou art worthy O Lord to receive glory and honor and power (1411 *dunamis*): for you have created (2936 *ktizo*—founded) all things (John 1:1–3; Col. 1:16; Heb. 1:2), and for thy pleasure they were created." **(Rev. 4:8–11)**

> We give thee thanks, O <u>Lord God Almighty</u> (Rev. 1:8, Rev. 4:8, Rev. 19:6), **which art, and was, and art to come**: because you have taken to thee thy great power (*dunamis*), and have reigned (Rev. 19:6). The nations were angry, and your wrath (Rev. 6:16–17; Rev. 14:18–20; Ps. 2:10–12) is come, and the time for judging the dead (Dan. 12:2; Isa. 26:19; 1 Thess. 4:14–16; Rev. 20:6; Phil. 3:11), and for rewarding your servants (Rev. 19:4–10), and for destroying those who destroy the earth (Rev. 19:1–2; Luke 18:7–8; Mal. 3:18). **(Rev. 11:17–18)**

Next: "Moses Wrote of Me"

CHAPTER 10

Moses Wrote of Me

For had you believed Moses, you would have believed me: for he wrote of me.

—John 5:46

Point no. 1: Jesus is the I AM.

Moses wrote the first five books of the Bible. Much of what we know about God is gleaned from Moses's writings, and most significant is the record of his first encounter with God. We find his first event recorded in Exodus chapter 3. Beginning at Exodus 3:1, here is what we learn:

1. The angel of the Lord appeared to Moses out of the midst of a burning bush (verse 2).
2. The angel of the Lord called to Moses out of the midst of the bush (verse 4).

3. God said, "I am the God of your father, the God of Abraham, Isaac, and Jacob" (verse 6).
4. I (God) have seen the affliction of my people, and <u>I have come down</u> to deliver them out of the hand of the Egyptians (verses 7 and 8).
5. Moses asked, "What is your name?" to which God replied, "I AM THAT I AM." This is my name forever. Tell them the "I AM" has sent you to them (verse 14–15).

The statement "I AM THAT I AM" says to us that God is self-sufficient, self-existent, and that he has no beginning or ending (Micah 5:2). In Revelation 22:13, Jesus said, "I am Alpha and Omega, the beginning and the end, the first and the last."

Jesus spoke these "I am" statements:

I (Jesus) <u>came down from heaven</u>, not to do my own will, but the will of him that sent me. (John 6:38)

I am the living bread <u>which came down</u> from heaven. (John 6:51)

Before Abraham was I am. (John 8:58; Exod. 3:14; Exod. 6:3; Gen. 15:1; Mic. 5:2)

I (Jesus) am the door of the sheep (Ps. 118:19–22). I am the good shepherd: The good shepherd gives his life for the sheep. (John 10:9–11)

I am the resurrection, and the life: He that believes into me though he were dead, yet shall he live: and whosoever lives and believes in me shall never die. (John 11:25–26)

You call me Master and Lord (Isa. 44:6–8; Rev. 1:17–18; Luke 6:46): and you say well for so I am. (John 13:13)

I am the way, the truth, and the life: no man (3762—nothing) comes to the Father, but through me. If you had known me, you would have known the Father also. (John 14:6–7)

Are you the Christ, the Son of the blessed? "I am," said Jesus. (Mark 14:61)

Point no. 2: Jesus is Lord (Yehovah).

Later in the early days of Moses's ministry in Exodus chapter 6, God revealed more about himself to Moses, stating the following:

1. I am Yehovah (the Lord) (Exod. 6:2).
2. I appeared to Abraham, Isaac, and Jacob by the name of <u>God Almighty</u>,* but by my name Yehovah (the Lord), I was not known to them (Exod. 6:3).
3. I am the Lord, your God (Exod. 6:7).

In Deuteronomy 6:4, Moses wrote, "Hear, O Israel: The Lord our God is one Lord."

Jesus said the following:

1. You call me Master and Lord: and you say well, for so I am (John 13:13).
2. Why call me, Lord, Lord, and do not the things which I say (Luke 6:46, Isa. 48:18)?

---

* In Exodus 6:3, the Lord said, "I (Yehovah) appeared as El Shadday (God Almighty), but by my name Yehovah (the Lord) I was not known." In the book of Revelation, the title "Lord God Almighty" is used and applied to Jesus.

3. I and my Father are one (John 10:30).

Note: It is written in Philippians chapter 2, verse 11 that a day is coming when every tongue will confess that Jesus Christ is Lord to the glory of God the Father.

Point no. 3: Jesus is a warrior.

After the parting of the Red Sea and the destruction of Pharaoh's army, Moses wrote in Exodus chapter 15, verse 3, "The Lord is a man of war." Today we emphasize the love of Jesus, but we fail to point out that he is a warrior and that a day is coming wherein he will come to deal with his adversaries and enemies. The prophet Isaiah says this about that day:

> Thus saith the Lord, the Lord of hosts, the mighty one of Israel, "I will ease me of mine adversaries, and avenge me of my enemies." (Isa. 1:24)

> According to their deeds he will repay: Fury to his adversaries, recompense to his enemies. (Isa. 59:18)

In the book of Revelation chapter 19, beginning at verse 11, we see the heavens opened and the Word of God coming with the armies of heaven to wage war on his enemies and to set up his kingdom upon the earth. In Revelation 6:15–17, the kings of the earth and the great men of this world are seen hiding in cliffs and in caves because the wrath of the Lamb has come upon them. The second psalm ends with this warning to the kings and judges of the earth: Kiss (fasten up to) the Son, lest he be angry, and you perish from the way, when his wrath is kindled, but a little (Rev. 6:16–17). Once again, we address the question: Who is the King of glory? He is the Lord, strong and mighty, the Lord, mighty in battle. The Lord of hosts—he is the King of glory (Ps. 24:8, 10).

Connecting the dots: From Moses's writings we've come to know:

1. Jesus is the I AM.
2. Jesus is Lord (Yehovah).
3. Jesus is a warrior, known as the Lord of hosts.
4. Jesus will ultimately deal with his adversaries and foes (Deut. 32:35).

Author's comment:

a. In Revelation 4:8–11, the title "Lord God Almighty" is given to the one that is and was and is to come to the one who sits upon the throne (Rev. 3:21), to the one who lives forever and ever (Rev. 1:18). He is the one who created all things (John 1:1–3; Col. 1:16; Heb. 1:2). *Jesus sits upon the throne, plus he is the one who lives forever and ever.*

b. In Revelation 11:17, after the sounding of the seventh trumpet (Rev. 11:15; 1 Cor. 15:51–52; Rev. 10:7), this title is again applied to the one who is, and was, and is to come: because now he has taken his great power and reigns (1 Tim. 6:15–16; Mic. 5:4; Ps. 97:1–6).

c. Revelation 15:3 presents the song of the Lamb and applies the title "Lord God Almighty" to the King of the saints (Jude 3; 1 Thess. 3:13; Rev. 19:11–16; Zech. 14:5; Rev. 17:14) before whom all nations shall come and worship (Isa. 2:1–4; Zech. 14:9; Dan. 7:14; Zech. 14:16). *Jesus is the Lamb plus the King of the saints.*

d. In Revelation 16:4–7, after the third vial of wrath is poured out, a voice out from the altar (Rev. 6:9–11) says, "True and righteous are your judgments, Lord God Almighty." *All judgments have been given to Jesus (John 5:22–23).*

Next: "The Lamb of God"

CHAPTER 11

The Lamb of God

The prophecy of the suffering Messiah, as found in Isaiah 53:7, speaks of the Messiah as a sheep, and Acts 8:32 directly applies Isaiah 53:7 to Jesus Christ. In John chapter 1, verse 29, John the Baptist introduced Jesus of Nazareth as the Lamb of God, which takes away the sin of the world. In 1 Peter 1:19, the apostle Peter referred to Jesus as a lamb without spot or blemish.

In the book of Revelation, the Lamb is spoken of in Revelation 5:6–13, Revelation 6:1, Revelation 6:16, Revelation 7:9–17, Revelation 12:11, Revelation 13:8, Revelation 14:1–10, Revelation 15:3, Revelation 17:14, Revelation 19:6–9, Revelation 21:1–9, Revelation 21:14, Revelation 21:22, Revelation 21:23, Revelation 21:27, and Revelation 22:1–3. The sheer number of times that this title, the Lamb, is used in the book of Revelation indicates its importance to us. Jesus is the main character in the book of Revelation (Rev. 1:1). It is well established in the Bible that Jesus Christ is the Lamb of God (Isa. 53:7–11; John 1:29; John 1:36; Acts 8:32–35; 1 Pet. 1:18–21). Here in Revelation, we see Jesus presented as a slain Lamb, receiving and opening the seven sealed scroll (Rev. 5:6–7; Rev. 6:1). We see multitudes of people in heaven worshipping the Lamb. We are warned to avoid the wrath of the Lamb. We see the marriage supper of the Lamb taking place in heaven. We see the Lamb's bride taking up residence in new Jerusalem. We are told that the Lamb is the light source for the new heaven and new earth. We are told that in the new heaven and new earth, God's dwelling place is with man, that the Lord God Almighty and the Lamb are the temple therein, and that the throne of God and the Lamb is there in the new Jerusalem.

Connecting the dots:

1. Jesus is the Lamb of God.
2. Jesus will reign throughout eternity with his Father.
3. Jesus has received a kingdom that cannot be destroyed (Dan. 7:14).

Author's notes:

Here, for your review, are the Revelation verses that speak to or speak of the Lamb (i.e., Rev. 5:6–13; Rev. 6:1; Rev. 6:16; Rev. 7:9–17; Rev. 12:11; Rev. 13:8; Revelation 14:1–10; Rev. 15:3; Rev. 17:14; Rev. 19:6–9; Rev. 21:1–9; Rev. 21:14; Rev. 21:22; Rev. 21:23; Rev. 21:27; and Rev. 22:1–3):

1. In Revelation 5:6–13, we first see a slain Lamb, standing in the midst of the throne and then standing off the throne in order to receive the seven sealed scroll. At the end of chapter 5, all creation is seen worshipping the one sitting upon the throne and the Lamb (John 3:13; John 6:62; John 8:19).
2. In Revelation 6:1, the Lamb opens the scroll by breaking the first seal.
3. In Revelation 6:16, the occupants of the earth reveal that the wrath of the Lamb has come (Ps. 2:12).
4. In Revelation 7:9–17, we see a great multitude of people standing before the Lamb. They are dressed in white robes, and we are told that they have washed their robes in the blood of the Lamb and have come out of great tribula-

tion (Matt. 24:21; Matt. 24:31; Rev. 14:12–16; 1 Thess. 4:14–17; 1 Cor. 15:51–52; Rev. 19:6–9; Rev. 11:15–17).

5. Revelation 12:11 tells us that we overcome Satan by the blood of the Lamb, by the word of our testimony, and by not loving our lives even unto death (Rev. 6:9–11; Rev. 21:7; Matt. 24:13; Luke 21:36).

6. Revelation 13:8 tells us that the Lamb was slain from the foundation of the world (2 Tim. 1:9; Eph. 1:4; 2 Thess. 2:13), and those individuals, whose names are not written in the Lamb's Book of Life, will worship the Antichrist during his reign on earth (Dan. 7:21–28; Rev. 13:7).

7. Revelation 14:1–10 speaks of the ministry of three angels, each of which gives warning to the occupants of the earth, telling them not to worship the Antichrist, not to buy into his economy, and not to take the mark of the beast. Those individuals who do so will suffer the wrath of God in the presence of the Lamb and experience the second death in the lake of fire (Matt. 25:41–46; Rev. 20:14).

8. In Revelation 15:3, we see a multitude of individuals in heaven who have overcome the Antichrist (Rev. 12:11; Rom. 8:38), and they are singing the song of Moses, the servant of God, and the song of the Lamb (Rev. 14:12).

9. Revelation 17:14 tells us that the Lamb is King of kings and Lord of lords.

10. Revelation 19:6–9 tells us that the marriage supper of the Lamb has come.

11. Revelation 21:1–9 discusses the new heaven and the new earth and places the Lamb's bride in the city of New Jerusalem.

12. Revelation 21:14 tells us that New Jerusalem has a foundation that's founded upon the twelve apostles of the Lamb (Eph. 2:20).

13. Revelation 21:22 tells us that there is no material (brick and mortar) temple in the city of New Jerusalem because the Lord God Almighty and the Lamb are its temple (Zech. 6:12; Eph. 2:19–22).

14. Revelation 21:23 tells us that there is no sun or moon necessary to provide light to the new earth because the Lamb is its light source (John 8:12; John 1:4).

15. Revelation 21:27 tells us that those who reside in the city of New Jerusalem are those individuals who have their names recorded in the Lamb's Book of Life (Rev. 13:8; Rev. 17:14; Rev. 12:11; 1 Pet. 1:2).

16. Revelation 22:1–3 tells us that the throne of God is the throne of the Lamb and that a pure river of water flows forth from this throne to water the tree(s) of life.

Author's comment:

Note that the Lamb in Revelation 5:6 has (2192—to hold, to possess) the seven spirits of God. In Revelation 1:4 and Revelation 4:5, we are told that the seven spirits are before the throne of God. In Revelation 3:1, Jesus tells us that he holds (2192) the seven spirits of God. In Matthew 3:11, John the Baptist tells us that Jesus will baptize individuals in the Holy Spirit (John 1:30–37). Jesus told his disciples that he would send the Holy Spirit to them from his Father (John 15:26; Acts 1:4–5). The first/initial outpouring of the Holy Spirit upon his disciples occurred on the day of Pentecost (fifty days after the crucifixion) in the city of Jerusalem and is recorded in Acts chapter 2, verses 1 through 42.

Next: "Coming and Going"

CHAPTER 12

Coming and Going

Jesus said, "No man (3762 *oudeis*—nothing, not even one) has ascended up into heaven, but he that came down out of heaven, even the Son of man who is in heaven.

—John 3:13

Here is what Jesus told us about <u>his first coming to earth</u> as the Son of Man:

1.) Jesus taught that he came down from heaven.

If I have told you earthly things and you believe not, how shall you believe, if I tell you of heavenly things? (John 3:12)

I (Jesus) came down from heaven, not to do my own will, but the will of him that sent me. (John 6:38)

No man has seen the Father, <u>but he which is of God</u>, he has seen the Father. (John 1:18; Exod. 33:18–21; 1 Cor. 10:4; John 6:46)

I am the living bread which came down from heaven: If any man eat of this bread (Luke 22:19), he shall live forever: and the bread that I will give for the life of the world is my flesh. (John 6:51; John 3:16)

What and if you shall see the Son of man ascend up to where he was before? (John 6:62; Acts 1:9–11; Phil. 2:7–8; John 1:14)

I am not come of myself, but he that sent me is true, whom you know not, but I know him: for I am from him, and he has sent me. (John 7:28–29)

You are from beneath; I am from above: you are of this world; I am not of this world. (John 8:23)

If God were your father, you (Pharisees) would love me (Jesus): for I proceeded forth (1831—to issue forth) and came from God; neither came I of myself, but he sent me. (John 8:42)

Before Abraham was I am. (John 8:58; Exod. 3:14; Exod. 6:3; Gen. 15:1; Mic. 5:2)

The Father himself loves you, because you have loved me, and have believed that I came out (1831—issued forth) from God. (John 16:27)

I came forth (1831—issued forth) from the Father, and came into the world: again, I leave the world, and go to the Father. (John 16:28)

And now, O Father, glorify me with your own self with the glory which I had with you before the world was. (Mic. 5:2–4; John 17:5)

2.) *Jesus told us that while he was here, he did the works of his Father.*

My food is to do the will of him that sent me, and to finish his work. (John 4:34; John 19:30)

My Father works hitherto, and I work. (John 5:17)

The Son can do nothing of himself, but what he sees the Father do. (Luke 5:17; John 5:19)

For the Father judges no man, but has committed all judgment to the Son: that all men should honor the Son, even as they honor the Father. (John 5:22–23)

I (Jesus) can of my own self do nothing: as I hear, I judge: and my judgment is just; because I seek not my own will, but the will of the Father who sent me. (Eph. 1:2–5; Eph. 1:9–12; Eph. 3:9–12; John 5:30)

The works which the Father has given me to finish (John 19:30), the same works that I do, bear witness of me, that the Father has sent me. (John 5:36)

I am come in my Father's name. (John 5:43)

My doctrine (1322—teaching) is not mine, but his that sent me. (John 7:16)

He that speaks of himself seeks his own glory: but he that seeks the glory of him that sent him is true. (John 7:18)

When you have lifted up the Son of Man, then shall you know that I am he (Deut. 18:18–19), and that I do nothing of myself; but as the Father has taught me, I speak these things, and he that sent me is with me: the Father has not left me alone: for I do always those things that please him. (John 8:28–29)

The works that I do in my Father's name, they bear witness of me. (John 10:25)

I have not spoken of myself; but the Father which sent me, he gave me a commandment, what I should say, and what I should speak... even as the Father said unto me so I speak. (Deut. 18:18; John 12:49–50)

all things that I have heard of my Father I have made known to you. (John 15:15)

3.) *Jesus taught that he came to earth in order to lay down his life for mankind.*

This is the work of God, that you believe into him whom he has sent. (John 6:29)

I (Jesus) am the door of the sheep (Ps. 118:19–22). I am the good shepherd: The good shepherd gives his life for the sheep. (John 10:9–11)

As the Father knows me, even so I know the Father: and I lay down my life for the sheep. (John 10:15)

My Father loves me, because I lay down my life, that I might take it up again (Rev. 1:17–18). No man (3762 *oudeis*—nothing) takes it from me, but I lay it down of myself. I have power (1849 *exousia*—authority) to lay it down, and I have power (authority) to take it again. This commandment I have received of my Father. (John 10:17–18)

For I came not to judge the world, but to save the world. (John 12:47)

4.) *Jesus told us that in him was eternal life.*

For God (John 8:54) so loved the world that <u>he gave</u> his only begotten (3439 *monogenes*—the only generated, or solely generated) Son; that whosoever believed into him should not perish but have eternal life. (John 3:16)

For as the Father has life in himself; so has he given to the Son to have life in himself. (John 1:4; Rev. 1:18; John 11:25–26; John 5:26)

And this is the will of the Father, that everyone which sees the Son, and believes into him, may have eternal life: and I will raise him up at the last day. (John 6:40)

I am the living bread which came down from heaven: If any man eat of this bread (Luke 22:19), he shall live forever: and the bread that I will give for the life of the world is my flesh. (John 6:51; John 3:16)

I am the resurrection, and the life: He that believes into me though he were dead, yet shall he live: and whosoever lives and believes in me shall never die. (John 11:25–26)

This is eternal life (1 John 5:11–13), that they might know you, the only true God, and Jesus Christ, whom you have sent. (John 17:3)

5.) *Jesus taught that he was in the Father and the Father was in him.*

If you had known me, you would have known my father also. (John 8:19)

If I honor myself, my honor is nothing: It is my Father that honors me; of whom you say that he is your God. (John 8:54)

My Father, which gave them me, is greater than all... I and my Father are one. (John 5:18; John 10:29–30)

If I do not the works of my Father, do not believe in me. But if I do...know and believe: the Father is in me, and I in him. (2 Cor. 5:19; John 10:37–38)

He that believes into me, believes not into me, but into him that sent me. He that sees me sees him that sent me. (John 12:44–45)

I am the way, the truth, and the life: no man (3762—nothing) comes to the Father, but through me. If you had known me, you would have known the Father also. (John 14:6–7)

He that has seen me has seen the Father (Col. 1:15; Heb. 1:2–3)... I am in the Father and the Father is in me...the Father that dwells in me, he does the works. (John 14:9–10)

He that hates me, hates my Father also. (John 15:23)

All things that the Father has are mine. (Matt. 11:27; Matt. 28:18–20; John 16:15)

Here is what Jesus told us about his going back to heaven to be with his Father:

1.) Jesus told us that he came from the Father and was returning to the Father and that in laying down his life for us, he was returning to the glory that he previously had in heaven with God, his Father.

Yet a little while am I with you, and then I go to him that sent me. (John 7:33–34)

The hour is come, that the Son of man should be glorified. (Dan. 7:13–14; Ps. 110:1; John 12:23)

Now is the Son of man glorified (John 12:23), and God is glorified in him. If God is glorified in him (in the Son of man) God shall also glorify him in himself, and glorify him at once. (Dan. 7:13–14; John 20:17; Heb. 1:8; Rev. 1:10–20; John 13:31–32)

Where I am going (Heb. 1:3), you cannot follow me now; but you shall follow me afterwards. (1 Cor. 15:23; John 13:36)

You have heard me say to you, that I go away and come again to you… I go to the Father: for the Father is greater than I. (John 14:28)

But now I go my way to him that sent me. (John 16:5)

I go to the Father. (John 16:16)

I came forth (1831—issued forth) from the Father, and came into the world: again, I leave the world, and go to the Father. (John 16:28)

Father, the hour is come; glorify your Son, that your Son also may glorify you. (John 17:1)

And now, O Father, glorify me with your own self with the glory which I had with you before the world was. (Mic. 5:2–4; John 17:5)

I ascend (John 6:62) to my Father, and to your Father (Matt 6:9); and to my God and your God (Dan. 7:13–14; Acts 1:9–11; Heb. 1:3). (John 20:17)

2.) *Jesus told his disciples that it was to their advantage that he return to the Father, for then the Holy Spirit would come to them.*

I will pray the Father, and he shall give you another Comforter, who will abide with you forever. (John 14:16)

But when the Comforter is come whom I will send to you from the Father (Acts 2:33; Matt 3:11), even the Spirit of truth which proceeds (1607—to come forth, come out of) from the Father (Rev. 3:1; Rev. 4:5; Rev. 5:6), he shall testify of me. (John 15:26)

If I go not away the Comforter will not come to you, but if I depart, I will send him to you. (John 16:7)

3.) *Jesus taught that the Holy Spirit would help the disciple to abide in him and do the works that he did.*

The works that I do shall ye also do. (John 14:12)

The Holy Spirit of truth; whom the world cannot receive because it sees him not...he dwells with you and shall be in you. (John 14:17)

In that day (Acts 2:1–4) you shall know that I am in my Father, you are in me, and I am in you (Eph. 4:6). (John 14:20)

If a man loves me, he will keep my words (Matt. 7:24): and my Father will love him, and we will come to him and make our abode (residence) with him. (John 14:23)

Abide in me, and I in you… Without me you can do nothing. (John 15:4)

If you abide in me, and my words abide in you, whatever you determine ask and it shall come into being. (John 15:7)

Whatsoever you ask the Father in my name, he will give… Ask and you shall receive. (John 16:23–24)

Here is what Jesus told us about his return to earth (his second coming):

For the Father judges no man, but has committed all judgment to the Son: that all men should honor the Son, even as they honor the Father. (John 5:22–23)

For as the Father has life in himself; so has he given to the Son to have life in himself. (John 1:4; Rev. 1:18; John 11:25–26; John 5:26)

And this is the will of the Father, that everyone which sees the Son, and believes into him, may have eternal life: and I will raise him up at the last day. (John 6:40)

you believe in God, believe also in me.
In my Father's house are many rooms... I go
to prepare a place for you... <u>I will come again</u>
(Matt. 24:30), and receive you to myself (Luke
17:34–37), that where I am, there you may be
also. (John 14:1–3)

I will not leave you comfortless: I will come
to you. (John 14:18)

And the high priest asked Jesus, "Are you
the Christ, the Son of the Blessed?" To which
Jesus said, "I am: and you shall see the Son of
man sitting on the right hand of power, and coming in the clouds of heaven." (Mark 14:61–62)

And then shall appear the sign of the Son of
man in heaven: and then shall all the tribes of the
earth mourn, and they shall see the Son of man
coming in the clouds of heaven with power and
great glory. (Matt. 24:30)

As you Father are in me, and I in thee, that
they may be one in us... And the glory which
you gave me I have given to them; that they may
be one, even as we are one. I in them, and you
in me, that they may be made perfect in one...
Father, I will that they also be with me where I
am (Luke 23:43); that they may behold my glory
which you gave me before the foundation of the
world (2 Tim. 1:9; Eph. 1:4). (John 17:21–24)

Here is what his apostles taught about his second coming:

> Looking for that blessed hope, and the glorious appearing of the great God and our savior Jesus Christ. (Mark 14:61–62; Titus 2:13)

> We beseech you, brethren, by the coming of our Lord Jesus Christ, and our gathering together unto him. (Matt. 24:30–31; 2 Thess. 2:1)

> When the Lord Jesus Christ shall be revealed from heaven with his mighty angels, in flaming fire, taking vengeance on them that know not God, and that obey not the gospel of our Lord Jesus Christ. (Ps. 97:1–3; 2 Thess. 1:7–8)

> For we know that when he shall appear we shall be like him. (1 John 3:2; Col. 3:4)

> at the coming of our Lord Jesus Christ with all his saints. (Zech. 14:5; 1 Thess. 3:13)

<u>Connecting the dots:</u>

1. Jesus taught that he came down from heaven.
2. Jesus taught that the God that the Jewish people believed in was his Father.
3. Jesus taught that he came to lay down his life for mankind.
4. Jesus taught that he came to give eternal life.
5. Jesus taught that he was in the Father, and the Father was in him.
6. Jesus taught that he was going back to his Father.
7. Jesus taught that in his place, he would send the Holy Spirit.

8. Jesus taught that the Holy Spirit would inhabit and empower his disciples.
9. Jesus taught that in the future, he would return to earth.

Next: "I Will Return to My Place"

I Will Return to My Place

In John 16:28, Jesus said, "I came forth (1831—issued forth) from the Father, and came into the world: again, I leave the world, and go to the Father." Psalm 110:1 tells us that the Adon prophesied to come—in Malachi 3:1, will sit at the right hand of God—until his enemies are made into a footstool for his feet. A prophecy in Hosea 5:15 reads, "I will go and return to my place, till they acknowledge their offence, and seek my face: In their affliction they will seek me early." In Isaiah 26:21 it is written, "Behold, the Lord comes out of his place to punish the inhabitants of the earth for their iniquity." In John 14:3, Jesus said to his church, "I will come again, and receive you to myself, that where I am, there you may be also." But you shall not see me (Jesus) again, until you (citizens of Jerusalem) meet this condition and say, "Blessed is he that comes in the name of the Lord" (Matt. 23:37–39). In prophecy, we see this condition being met by Israel in Psalm 118:16–26 which reads, "The right hand of the Lord is exalted, the right hand of the Lord does valiantly. I (Israel) shall not die, but live, and declare the works of the Lord. The Lord has chastened me sore (Jer. 30:7–8): but he has not given me over to death. Open to me the gates of righteousness, and I will go into them, and I will praise the Lord… I will praise thee, for you have heard me, and you have become my salvation. The stone which the builders rejected is become the head corner stone. This is the Lord's doing; and it is marvellous in our eyes. This is the day which the Lord has made; we will rejoice and be glad in it. Save now, I beseech thee, O Lord: O Lord, I beseech you, break forth now. <u>Blessed is he that comes in the name of the Lord</u>."

You might ask why. Why must Israel cry out to the Lord, requesting that he again send the Adon? It is because, when Jesus desired to gather together Israel to himself, the nation was unwilling to have him rule over them (John 19:15). In fact, he was rejected by the national leaders (Isa. 53:3; Ps. 118:22–23) and the people of Jerusalem (Matt. 27:22–25). Therefore, Jesus established the condition that Israel would not see him again, until they say, "<u>Blessed is he that comes in the name of the Lord</u>" (Matt. 23:37–39).

We know from prophecy that the nation of Israel will cry out to the Lord, and in that day, the Lord will physically return to fight and protect the city of Jerusalem and his people, Israel, for it is written, "In that day shall the Lord defend the inhabitants of Jerusalem... As the angel of the Lord before them. And it shall come to pass in that day, that I will seek to destroy all the nations that come against Jerusalem. And I will pour upon the house of David, and upon the inhabitants of Jerusalem, the spirit of grace and supplication: And they shall look upon me whom they have pierced, and they shall mourn for him, as one mourns for his only son" (Zech. 12:8–10).

Author's comment no. 1:

Psalm 118 lays out the methodology under which Israel came to the realization that they had missed out on receiving their Messiah and in turn receive Jesus Christ as their Lord and God. The methodology cited in Psalm 118 goes like this:

1. Israel in distress will call upon the Lord (Jer. 30:3–7).
2. The Lord will put them in a large place (Matt. 24:16; Rev. 12:14).

3. Israel will receive a little help possibly from the Christian church (Mic. 5:3) (verse 7).
4. Israel comes to realize that it cannot trust in men or in the princes of this earth (verse 8 and 9).
5. Israel finds itself surrounded on all sides by enemies and is forced to defend herself (verse 10–13).
6. Israel comes to realize that her salvation (safety) rests only with the Lord (Exod. 15:2).
7. The angel of the Lord goes forth with the army of Israel (Zech. 12:8; Mic. 7:15–17; Joel 2:30).
8. The Jewish people realize that the Lord has chastened them for their rejection of Jesus Christ (verse 18).
9. They ask the Lord to open the gates of righteousness so that they may enter in (John 10:9; John 8:24).
10. They acknowledge that the Lord has become their salvation (verse 21).
11. They realize that the stone, which the builders of Judaism rejected, is the head corner stone (verse 22).
12. They ask the Lord to break through now in order to make them safe (verse 25) (Isa. 26:21).
13. They call upon the name of Jesus, saying, "Blessed is he that comes in the name of the Lord."
14. They acknowledge in praise that God is the Lord (John 20:28; Deut. 6:4; John 13:13).
15. They give thanks, "for his mercy endures forever."

Author's comment no. 2:

When Jesus returned to his Father, he returned to his place of former residence (John 1:18), the difference being that he now resides there (in the bosom of the Father) with a new additional nature—that of a glorified man—and he resides there, waiting for his enemies to be made into a footstool for his feet. At the chosen time (Acts 1:7), the Father will send him again to the earth. His first assignment is to gather his church from the earth (Titus 2:13). This gathering of the church is a parousia (3952), a coming near. In it, Jesus appears in the sky, but he does not come physically to the earth (Matthew 24:30). For the church, the day of the parousia is known as the day of redemption (Rom. 8:23), for this is the day that believing Christians, both living and dead, receive their glorified bodies (1 Cor. 15:49). This day is also commonly called the day of rapture (1 Thess. 4:14–17), and its occurrence causes Israel to acknowledge and receive Jesus Christ as their Redeemer and Lord (Ps. 97:10; Isa. 44:6). Following the removal of the church, all surviving Israel will be saved (Rom. 11:25–26; Zech. 13:8–9; Joel 2:32), and they will fight against the Antichrist (Zech. 12:8; Zech. 14:14). Also, at this time, the wrath of God will be poured out upon the earth, resulting in the battle of Armageddon (Revelation 16:16). In this last battle, Jesus Christ comes physically to earth (Zech. 14:4; Acts 1:11–12) with an army composed of his saints (Zech. 14:5). In this battle, all his enemies will be present on the earth. This includes the demons and fallen angels that were loosened from the abyss at the fifth trumpet (Rev. 9:1–11), the principalities, and powers of darkness that resided in heaven (Eph. 6:12) until they were cast out just prior to the rapture (Matt. 24:29) and the human armies of the Antichrist (Rev. 19:17–21). The battle of Armageddon begins at Jerusalem (Zech. 14:1–5; Joel 2:1) but moves to an area, north and west of the city (Dan. 11:45). The battle may last as long as forty-five days (Dan. 12:11–12), but in the end, Jesus Christ will begin his earthly reign upon the throne of David (Dan. 7:22; Luke 1:32). The demons, the fallen angels, the principalities and powers of darkness, the Antichrist, and his false prophet will be thrown into Gehenna (Matt. 25:41; Rev. 19:20). Satan will be thrown into the abyss (Rev. 20:1–3), and the human armies of the Antichrist will be utterly destroyed (Rev. 19:21). At this point in time, the millennial reign of Christ begins, and there will be peace on the earth (Rev. 20:6; Mic. 5:4; Zeph. 3:15).

Connecting the dots:

1. Jesus returned to heaven and sits in the heavenlies with his Father (Eph. 1:20; Ps. 110:1).
2. Jesus will come again for his church (John 14:3; 2 Thess. 2:1; 1 Thess. 4:16–17; 1 Cor. 15:51–52).

3. Jesus will come again to destroy his enemies (Zech. 14:1–5; Ps. 110:5–6; Luke 18:7; Isa. 47:3–4).
4. Jesus will sit on the throne of David and reign over all the earth (Luke 1:32; Dan. 7:14; Ps. 47:2; Rev. 20:4–6).
5. When Jesus reigns, Israel will live in peace and be secure (Zeph. 3:14–15; Isa. 2:3–4; Mic. 4:1–4).

Next: "The Wrath of God"

CHAPTER 14

The Wrath of God

Understand this:

> For the wrath of God comes upon the children of disobedience. (Col. 3:6)

and

> God shall send upon them that believed not the truth; a strong delusion (4106—something that deceives or misleads), <u>and they will believe a lie</u>. (2 Thess. 2:10–12)

but

> We wait for his Son from heaven: he delivers us from the wrath to come. (1 Thess. 1:10; Rom. 5:9)

and

> God will avenge his own elect. (Col. 3:12;
> Luke 18:7; Ps. 97:10)

Psalm 83 speaks of a time when the world will turn against both Israel and the Church.

> **O God, do not keep silence; do not hold thy peace or be still.**
> **For lo, your enemies are in tumult (commotion); those that hate you have raised their heads.**
> **They lay crafty plans against your people; they consult together against your hidden ones (your church). (Ps. 91:1; Col. 3:4)**
>
> **They say, "Come, let us wipe them out as a nation; let the name of Israel be remembered no more."**
> **Yes, they conspire with one accord; against you they make a covenant. (Ps. 83:1–5)**

Point no. 1

The wrath (anger) of God shall come upon them that choose not to believe the gospel of truth (Eph. 1:13) but have decided instead to believe a lie. And as one does this, God allows him/her to become delusional in their reasoning ability (2 Thess. 2:10–12). Today, there are so many lies circulating in our society as truth that we need to ask ourselves, What controls and motivates us in our daily lives? Are we living a lie? We really need to identify the passionate hot-button issues that control the strong emotions within us, for our emotions often allow us to make untruths into certifiable truths. Recall that Jesus said, "Everyone that is of the truth hears my voice" (John 18:37). What voice is our society listening to? This is important because Jesus also said, "If anyone is not with me, he is against me: and he that is against me scatters" (Luke 11:23). Are we in opposition to Christ? Do we stand against the Lord of hosts? It may be wise, at this time, to also ask yourself this question: "Who am I gathering with, and who am I serving" (Mal. 3:14–18)? If we answer these questions, we may discover that we are serving ourselves (2 Tim. 3:1–5) or perhaps come to see that we are serving and worshipping the things created (the world) rather than the one who created them (Rom. 1:25).

Psalm 2 also tells of a coming world rebellion and gives warning to its leaders:

> Why do the Gentiles rage, and the community of God imagine a vain thing?
>
> The kings of the earth set themselves, and the rulers take counsel together against the Lord and his Messiah saying, Let us break their bands asunder, and cast away their cords from us.
>
> He that sits in the heavens shall laugh, the Lord shall have them in derision: He shall speak unto them in his wrath, and vex them in his sore displeasure. I have set my king upon my holy hill of Zion, he says. (Matt. 27:37)
>
> I (Jesus) will declare the decree: The Lord has said unto me, "Thou art my Son; this day have I begotten thee." (Matt. 3:17; Matt. 17:5)
>
> Ask of me, and I will give thee the Gentiles for your inheritance, and the uttermost parts of the earth for your possession. You shall break them with a rod of iron; you shall dash them in pieces like a potter's vessel.
>
> Be cautious therefore, ye kings: Accept instruction, ye judges (rulers) of the earth. Serve the Lord with reverence, and rejoice with trembling. Kiss (5401—to fasten up to) the Son, lest

he be angry, and you perish from the way, when his wrath is kindled but a little. Blessed are all they that put their trust in him (Heb. 10:37–39). (**Ps. 2**)

Point no. 2

We are in an era in which many have decided to tear down and throw away our Western culture. A culture founded upon biblical principles and the teachings of Jesus Christ. Many desire to do this because they find our cultural norms too restrictive, and they believe that they can undo them. They have reasoned that since man has installed them that their own men (those of their persuasion) can simply change them to their liking. Regarding this assumed position, Psalm 2 tells us that the Lord laughs at their naivete. It tells us that the Lord shall have them in derision, that he will be angry with them, and that he will discomfort them. Notice also that he warns the kings, judges, and rulers that they have installed to be cautious and careful not to anger the Son, not even a little (Rev. 6:16)!

Nevertheless, the following scriptures found in the book of Revelation indicate that the end-time generation will not heed the warning:

> The nations were angry, and <u>your wrath has come</u>...and the time is come to destroy those which corrupt the earth.* (Rev. 11:18)

> And he (Jesus) treads the winepress of the wrath of Almighty God. (Rev. 19:15; Rev. 14:15–20)

> And they (the kings of the earth, the great men of the earth) said to the mountains and

---

* **Regarding the corrupters of the earth: Where are the great influencers of our day taking us? Revelation 11:18 states that the time is come to destroy those who are destroying (1311—to ruin, to corrupt) the earth.**

rocks, "Fall on us, and hide us from the face of him that sits on the throne, and from <u>the wrath of the Lamb</u>: For the great day of his wrath is come, and who shall be able to stand?" (Rev. 6:15–17)

And Psalm 110:5–6 also tells us the following:

- The Lord at your right hand shall strike through kings in the day of his wrath (verse 5).
- He shall judge among the Gentiles. He shall fill places with dead bodies (Rev. 19:21; Ezek. 39:17–22; Rev. 14:19–20); he shall wound the heads over many lands (verse 6).

<u>Connecting the dots:</u>

1. The wrath of God will come upon those who refuse to receive the love of Christ (2 Thess. 2:10).
2. Jesus says that whosoever is against him will be scattered (Luke 11:23).
3. In wrath (anger) will he speak to his enemies (Ps. 2:5; Isa. 59:17–18).
4. The prudent man will kiss (fasten up to) the Son lest he be angry, and you perish from the way (Ps. 2:12; John 14:6).

Author's comment:

The Father's plan for eternity is to unite all things in Christ, the things in heaven and in earth (Eph. 1:10). Therefore, he that makes himself an adversary of Christ stands in opposition to God's plan and purpose for mankind and sits on the wrong side of history. In Isaiah 1:24, the Lord says that he will ease himself of his adversaries (6862—opponents) and avenge himself of his enemies (341—haters). He says that he will repay his foes according to their deeds, fury for his adversaries, recompense for his enemies (Isa. 59:18). Yet vengeance is not a necessity, for God has made a way of escape (John 3:16). He has not appointed us to wrath but to the obtaining of salvation through our Lord Jesus Christ (1 Thess. 5:9). The Bible tells us that those believing on the Lord Jesus Christ shall be saved from the wrath of God (John 3:16–21; Rom. 5:9).

The word *corrupt* comes from a Latin word that means "to break." A corrupter is a person who has decided to break the bands that God has created to govern his creation, and to throw them aside so that he/she can freely make decisions that are incorrect and contrary to the will of God.

Those seeking to break the bands and cast away the foundational cords that tie us to the God of the Bible are faced with a dilemma: They must redefine good as evil and make evil appear good (Isa. 5:20). In order to achieve this task, they have cast aspersions and trampled down truth in the marketplace (media) of public consumption (Isa. 59:13–18). Those doing this lack the foresight to know that their efforts will only return us to a period of time that approximates the days of Noah. During those days, prior to the flood, it is recorded that man's every thought was on evil (Gen. 6:5), and little do they understand that the recklessness that they are releasing upon society will affect them also (Isa. 3:11). Today, all that we see developing before our very eyes aligns well with what Jesus said about the days preceding his second coming. We find Jesus's prediction in Luke 17:26, which reads, "As it was in the days of Noah, so shall it be also in the days of the Son of man." Speaking of those days, Genesis chapter 6, verse 5 states, "The wickedness of man was great and every imagination of man's heart was only evil continually." Again, speaking of the days prior to his return, Jesus stated that because lawlessness abounds, the love of many will wax cold (Matt. 24:12). The deconstruction of Western culture is at the direction of the prince of darkness. His intent and purpose are not simply the destruction of the Western nations and their culture but to pave the way for the coming of his Antichrist (John 5:43; Dan. 7:21; Rev. 13:4–8) and the attempted destruction of the church of Christ (Matt. 16:18). In Daniel chapter 12, verse 7, the angel told the prophet Daniel that when he (Satan) shall have accomplished to scatter the power of the holy people (the saints) (Dan. 8:24; Rev. 13:7), all these things (all that you have seen) shall be finished. Satan's current woke attack against the church has just begun. I expect that it will pick up speed and become more intense, leading to the great apostasy spoken of in 2 Thessalonian 2:3 and Luke 18:8. Interestingly enough, this will occur just before Jesus Christ comes to gather together his church to himself (2 Thess. 2:1; Titus 2:13; Rev. 14:14–15). The parable of the ten virgins reminds us to stay on guard (1 Cor. 16:13–14) and to be ready for Christ's coming (parousia), for when the door is shut, it is shut (Matt. 25:10–12). Therefore, Christian, stay awake, stand fast in the faith. Do not quit, be strong, and let everything you do be done in love (1 Cor. 16:13–14).

Next: "The Day of the Lord"

CHAPTER 15

The Day of the Lord

> Whom did you dread and fear, so that you lied, and did not remember me, did not even give me a thought. Have I not held my peace, even for a long time, and so you do not fear me?
>
> —Isaiah 57:11

> These things you have done and I have been silent; you thought that I was one like yourself, but now I rebuke you, and lay the charge before you.
>
> —Psalm 50:21

The day of the Lord (Isa. 13:6; Joel 2:31) is also known as the day of the Lord of hosts (Isa. 2:12). It is the day in which the Lord comes to the earth in order to deal with his adversaries and foes. The day of the Lord begins with the rapture (gathering) of the church at the sounding of the seventh trumpet (Rev. 11:15). Right before the seventh trumpet sounds (Rev. 10:7), the two slain witnesses stand up and ascend into heaven. Then those who have survived the great tribulation (Matt. 24:15–29) shall be caught up, together with the two witnesses, to meet the Lord in the air (1 Thess. 4:14–17; Matt. 24:30–31; 1 Cor. 15:51–52). Then, with the church removed from the earth, the seven vials of God's wrath (anger) are poured out upon the earth. Of particular interest to us are the sixth and seventh vials. The sixth vial (Rev. 16:12–16) attracts and encourages the kings of the east to come for war into the land of Israel (Zech. 14:1–2; Joel 3:2). The seventh vial culminates in the battle of Armageddon, and it ends with a great hailstorm (Rev. 16:21; Rev. 11:19). This is the day whereof I have spoken, says the Lord God (Ez. 39:8; Rev. 16:17).

Here is what we know about the day of the Lord:

1. It occurs after the church is removed from the earth.
2. Based on Daniel 12:11–12, it may not be a single twenty-four-hour day. It may be a length of time, possibly for-ty-five days long.
3. Prior to the day of the Lord of hosts, all nations will come against Jerusalem to battle. Jerusalem shall be taken, and half of the city shall go forth into captivity (Zech. 14:2; Joel 3:3). Judah, with the help of the Lord, shall also fight at Jerusalem against the nations (Zech. 12:8). It is at this time that the Lord shall stand upon the Mount of Olives and bring all his saints (Jude 3; Eph. 4:12) with him to do battle (Zech. 14:5). The battle for Jerusalem is recorded in Joel chapter 2, verses 1 through 11. Many people believe that these verses in Joel are about a great plague of locusts; however, I believe that verse 8 speaks of Christ's army, which is made up of his saints (Reve. 19:14; Rev. 17:14). I say this because Joel 2:8 reads, "And when they fall upon the sword, they shall not be wounded." Why? Because the

rapture has previously happened, and like Christ, these soldiers, who return from heaven with Christ, can no longer be wounded or die, for they are in their glorified, resurrected bodies (Rom. 8:23). It is this battle over Jerusalem that causes the Antichrist to stop his pillaging of Egypt and return to the land of Israel (Dan. 11:44). It is written in Daniel chapter 11, verse 45 that he (Antichrist) will withdraw his troops from Egypt and travel north and east and then pitch his tent between the seas and come to his end there, with no one to help him (Dan. 11:45).

4. Regarding the battle of Armageddon, the prophet Micah added this (Mic. 7:15–20): God will do marvellous things (Joel 2:30), things that will remind the Jewish people of their exodus under Moses's direction (Zech. 12:8). The attacking nations shall be confounded and in fear of the God of Jacob (Ps. 46:6–11). The Lord will keep his covenant with Jacob (Gen. 35:10–15; Rom. 11:28).

5. Here is what the prophet Ezekiel says about that day (Ez. 38:17–23). Remember: All nations will be there in the valley of decision (Joel 3:14–16), fighting against Israel and Jerusalem, and that includes the land of Gog (Russia). On that day, in the land of Israel, there will be a great shaking, a great earthquake (Rev. 16:18). Every man's sword shall be against his brother. God will rain great hailstones upon the attacking nations, and they will come to know that I (Jesus) am the Lord.

6. To this, the prophet Zechariah added (Zech. 14:12–13) that there shall be a great confusion among the attacking nations. They shall fight among themselves and kill each other. Moreover, the Lord shall send a plague among them, causing their flesh to melt off their bodies, their eyes to melt away in their eye sockets, and their tongues to dissolve away in their mouths.

7. When the battle of Armageddon is complete, the following will have been accomplished:
    a) The Antichrist and his false prophet will be thrown into the lake of fire (Gehenna) (Rev. 19:20), which is defined as the second death (Rev. 20:14).
    b) Satan will be thrown into the abyss (Rev. 20:3).
    c) The birds of the air will feast upon the dead bodies of the attacking nations (Rev. 19:21; Ezek. 39:17–22).
8. Having seen the workings of God against his enemies, the people remaining on the earth will be meek and humble (Zeph. 3:12; Matt. 5:5). Jesus, according to his Father's plan, will sit upon the throne of David (Luke 1:32; Zech. 6:12–13). The kingdom promised to Israel will come into being (Isa. 2:2; Mic. 5:2; Acts 3:21; Matt. 19:28). The land promised to the patriarchs of Israel shall be given to the people of Israel (Jer. 23:6–8; Jer. 16:15). Those Jewish people, who were sold into captivity (Joel 3:6), will be brought home to Israel (Isa. 11:11–12). The people of Israel will be safe and secure in their own land (Zeph. 3:15; Mic. 5:4), and there will be no more war on earth (Isa. 2:4).

Author's comment:

Why am I telling you these things about the day of the Lord of host? Because if you believe in God, you need to be on the right side of history. Even our brief review above, concerning the day of the Lord, warns us not to be on the wrong side. As we discussed in chapter 14, there are many influencers and leaders today who want to break God's bands asunder and throw away his chords. However, in order to do this, they have set out to corrupt society by teaching that right is wrong, and wrong is right, and by proclaiming that their motivations are highly virtuous, equitable, and fair. If you carefully observe their efforts and take time to connect the dots, you will realize that you don't want to go down their proposed path with them, as they are taking us directly into the day of the Lord. Considering the judgments that we have just seen associated with that day, it does not appear wise to go down that road and make oneself an adversary or enemy of Jesus Christ (Isa. 1:24; Isa. 59:18; Zech. 14:12–13). Besides, Jesus is our only way of escape from the wrath to come (1 Thess. 1:10), and only he has the keys that free us from hell and death (Rev. 1:17–18; Matt. 10:28).

<u>Connecting the dots</u>:

1. Receive the love of the truth (John 3:16), don't believe into the lies of Satan (2 Thess. 2:10–12).
2. The Lord will deal harshly with those that oppose him and hate him (Isa. 59:18; Isa. 1:24).

Next: "Thy Kingdom Come"

Thy Kingdom Come

When you pray, pray…thy kingdom come.

—Matt. 6:10

There are six prophecies **(Isa. 4:2–6; 11:1–16; Jer. 23:5–8, 33:14–17; Zech. 3:8–10; 6:12–13)** that speak of a coming kingdom and involve themselves with the branch of Jesse and/or the branch of David. This is significant because in the New Testament, the title "son of David" is directly applied to Jesus. (See Matthew 9:27; 12:23; 15:22; 20:30–31; 21:9; 21:15; 22:41–46; Mark 10:47–48; 12:35–37; Luke 18:38–39; 20:41–44; and John 7:42.) The use of this title, son of David, is made all the more important because of the dialogue recorded in Matthew 22:41–46 (Mark 12:35–37; Luke 20:41–44), which ties Jesus directly to Psalm 110:1 and reads as follows:

While the Pharisees were gathered together, Jesus asked them, "What do you think of the

Christ? Whose son is he?" They said to Jesus, "The son of David." To which Jesus replied, "Why then does David in the spirit call him Lord (Psalm 110). For if David calls him Lord, how is he his son?" And no man was able to answer this question. **(Matt. 22:41–46)**

The Lord (Yehovah) said to my Lord (Adon), sit thou at my right hand, until I make your enemies your footstool. **(Ps. 110:1)**

Isaiah 4:2–6, 11:1–16, Jeremiah 23:5–8, 33:14–17, Zechariah 3:8–10, 6:12–13 speak of the branch, and they read as follows:

In that day (1 Tim. 6:15–16; Rev. 11:15–17; Rev. 20:6) (i.e., the millennium) shall the Branch of the Lord (Yehovah) (John 10:30; 17:5) be beautiful and glorious (Mic. 5:4), and the fruit of the earth shall be excellent and comely (Rom. 8:19–23) for them that are escaped of Israel (Zech. 13:8–9; Joel 2:32; Jer. 16:14–15; Rom. 11:25–26; Ps. 118:18–27). And it shall come to pass, that he that is left in Zion and he that remains in Jerusalem (Rev. 11:13; Zech. 14:2) shall be called holy (Isa. 52:1–12; Zech. 14:21). **(Isa. 4:2–6)**

And there shall come forth a rod out of the stem of Jesse, and a Branch shall grow out of his roots (Isa. 53:10; 1 Cor. 15:20–23; Rev. 5:5–14; Matt. 16:18; Rev. 20:4–6; Rev. 1:6)…and it shall come to pass in that day, that the Lord shall set his hand again the second time to recover the remnant of his people (Zech. 13:8–9; Jer. 16:14–15) which shall be left, from Assyria, and from Egypt

(Joel 3:6)…and there shall be a highway for the remnant of his people, which shall be left, from Assyria; like it was to Israel in the days that he came up out of the land of Egypt. (Jer. 23:7–8; Zeph. 3:19–20; **Isa. 11:1–16)**

Behold, the days come, says Yehovah, that I will raise unto David a righteous Branch (Dan. 9:24), and a king (John 18:33–37; John 19:19; Ps. 2:6) shall reign and prosper, and execute judgment (Rev. 5:5; John 5:22–23) and justice in the earth (Ps. 97:1–2). In his day (1 Tim. 6:15–16) Judah shall be saved (3467—to be safe and secure), and Israel shall dwell safely (Mic. 5:4; Zeph 3:15): And this is his name whereby he shall be called, the Lord our Righteousness (Yehovah Tsedeq) (1 Cor. 1:30; Dan. 9:24)…and they shall no more say, "The Lord lives, who brought up the children of Israel out of the land of Egypt." But now they shall say, "The Lord (Yehovah) lives, who brought up and led the seed of the house of Israel out of the north country (Isa. 11:11), and from all the countries where he had driven them; and they shall dwell in their own land (1 Chron. 17:9; Gen. 15:18–21)." **(Jer. 23:5–8)**

Behold the days come (1 Tim. 6:15–16), says the Lord (Yehovah), that I will perform that good thing which I have promised unto the house of Israel and to the house of Judah (Acts 1:6; Rev. 11:15; Dan. 7:22; Luke 12:32; Rev. 20:4). In those days, and at that time, I will cause the Branch of righteousness to grow up unto David; and he shall execute judgment (Rev. 11:18; John 5:22–23; John 8:26; Isa. 2:4) and righteousness in the earth (Ps. 97:1–2). In these days (Rev. 11:17) shall Judah be saved (Rom. 11:25–26; Mic. 7:19–20; Joel 3:20–21; Mic. 5:3–4; Ps. 110:3; Ps. 118:18–29), and Jerusalem shall dwell safely (Isa. 2:1–4; Mic. 5:4; Zeph. 3:14–17)…and David shall never lack a man to sit upon the throne (1 Chron. 17:10–14; Matt. 19:28; Rev. 3:21; Rev. 20:6) of the house of Israel (Acts 1:6). **(Jer. 33:14–17)**

For behold, I (Yehovah) will bring forth my servant the Branch…and I will remove the iniquity of that land in one day (Matt. 23:34–39; Hos. 5:15–6:3; Isa. 40:1–2; Ps. 118:14–18; Zech. 12:8–13:1; Joel 2:32; Rom. 11:26–28; Mic. 7:18–20; Ps. 118:29)…in that day, says the Lord of hosts (Yehovah Tsava) (Mal. 3:1), you shall call every man your neighbor (Luke 10:29–37) under the vine and under the fig tree. **(Zech. 3:8–10)**

Thus saith the Lord of Hosts, "Behold the man whose name is the Branch, he shall grow up out of his place (Matt. 2:3–6; Heb. 10:5; Mic. 5:2), and he shall build the temple of the Lord (Acts 7:48; Acts 17:24; Eph. 2:21–22; Rev. 3:12), and he shall bear the glory (John 17:22–24), and sit and rule upon his throne (1 Chron. 17:11–15; Rev. 3:21; Matt. 19:28; Ps. 2:6; Dan. 7:13–14); and he shall be a priest upon his throne (Ps. 110:4): and the counsel of peace shall be between them both." **(Zech. 6:12–13)**

Comment no. 1

Notice how the above branch prophecies use the phrase "in that day" to refer to a coming kingdom of righteousness, peace, and safety for the nation of Israel. Note also how the following scriptures support and supplement our understanding of when that kingdom is to come.

Jesus said, "My time has not yet come." (John 7:6; John 2:4)

Jesus said to Pilate, "Presently my kingdom is not from hence (1782—on both sides)." (John 18:36)

In his time he (Jesus) shall show, who is the blessed and only potentate, the King of kings, and the Lord of lords (Rev. 19:16); the only one holding immortality (Rev. 1:18), and dwelling in light unapproachable. (1 Tim. 6:15–16)

The Lord (Yehovah) has taken away your judgments, he has cast out your enemies: The king of Israel, even the Lord (Yehovah) is in your midst: you shall not see evil any more. (Zeph. 3:15)

And he shall stand and feed in the strength of Yehovah, in the majesty of the name of the Lord his God (John 20:17); and they (Israel) shall abide: For now he shall be great unto the ends of the earth. (Mic. 5:4)

In the regeneration (3824—the new beginning, the reconstitution) when the Son of man sits in the throne of his glory (Mark 14:62), you shall sit upon twelve thrones judging the twelve tribes of Israel (Luke 12:32, Rev 20:6). (Matt. 19:28)

> And the Lord my God (Yehovah Elohiym)
> (Deut. 6:4) shall come, and all the saints (Jude
> 3; Eph. 4:12) with thee (Zechariah). (Zech 14:5)

> And the time came that the saints (Jude 3;
> Rom. 1:7; Eph. 4:12) possessed the kingdom.
> (Dan. 7:22)

> And they (saints) shall reign with him
> (Jesus) a thousand years. (Luke 12:32; Rev. 20:6)

Comment no. 2

The prophecies found in Isaiah 4:2–6; 11:1–16; Jeremiah 23:5–8; 33:14–17; Zech 3:8–10; 6:12–13 all concern the branch, the one who is of the lineage of David. It is for this reason that both Matthew and Luke, in their gospels, traced the lineage of Jesus Christ, the Son of Man, back to David. The genealogy presented in Matthew (Matthew 1:1–17) pertains to Joseph as the legal, rather than the natural, father of Jesus. The genealogy recorded in Luke (Luke 3:23–38) belongs to Mary because Jesus did not have a natural father (Luke 1:26–38) but was conceived of the Holy Spirit, and therefore, being born of a woman, he can be known as both the Son of Man and the Son of God (Luke 1:32–33).

Note: The two prophecies in Isaiah speak of a day wherein the branch (son of David) will reign over a recovered remnant of the Jewish population. The day spoken of in these two prophecies point toward the time period which we commonly refer to as the millennial reign of Christ or simply: the millennium (Rev. 20:1–7). The two prophecies in Jeremiah tell us that the branch will rule as a king and that during his reign the nation of Israel shall dwell securely in their own land. These two prophecies also tell us that during his reign, the Lord shall bring the captives of Israel out of the North country and resettle them in the land promised to their forefathers (Rom. 11:28; Gen. 15:18–21). The kingdom established will be the righteous and equitable kingdom that Israelis have desired to see and have sought after for centuries (Acts 1:6). Note that during this time, David will never lack a man to sit upon his throne because the resurrected Jesus Christ (the one who was and is and is to come) cited in these prophecies has indeed come, and he lives forevermore (Rev. 1:17–18). Lastly, the two prophecies in Zechariah tell us that the branch of David, the servant of Yehovah, shall remove the iniquity of the land in one day (John 19:14–16; 10:17–18; Heb. 1:3), that he shall grow up in the land of Israel (Isa. 53:1–12), and that he shall build the temple of the Lord (Eph. 2:20–22). They further state that in his day (1 Tim. 6:15–16), he shall be glorious and sit and rule upon his throne as both king and priest (Ps. 110:4).

Comment no. 3

The Hebrew word *messiah* means "anointed one." In the Old Testament, the title "Messiah" was given to the one who was to reign and rule over the kingdom of David. The Messiah was to be of the lineage of David (Jer. 23:5), and he was to put an end to sin (Zech. 3:9) and to war (Isa. 2:4) and put into place a kingdom founded upon peace (Isa. 11:6–9) and righteousness (Jer. 23:6). In the Old Testament, the actual word *messiah* is only used in Daniel chapter 9. In the New Testament the title "Messiah" is used twice: once in John 1:41 and once in John 4:25. Its application in both of these verses is significant because they equate the Hebrew word *messiah* to the Greek word *Christ* and indicate that the word *Christ* and the word *messiah* are interchangeable. In Matthew 1:16–17, the title "Christ" is specifically applied to Jesus, the Son of Mary. Some individuals have said that Jesus never stated that he was the Messiah, but that statement is incorrect. In John 4:25–26, Jesus clearly disclosed that he is indeed the promised Messiah. It must be understood that his promised kingdom is yet to come (Matt. 6:10; John 18:33–40; Mark 14:61–64; Matt. 24:30–31; Ps. 97:10–12; Rev. 11:15). Revelation 20:6 reads, "Blessed and holy is he that has part in the first resurrection (Phil. 3:11)…for they shall reign with Christ a thousand years." In Matthew 6:10, Jesus tells us to pray for his coming kingdom, and the book of Revelation (Rev. 22:17) concludes announcing that the Spirit and the bride say, "Come."

<u>Connecting the dots</u>:

1. Jesus is the Son of David.
2. Jesus is the Son of Man.
3. Jesus is Messiah.
4. There is coming a day when…
5. Jesus is King.
6. Israel will live in the land of promise.
7. Jesus will sit upon the throne of David and reign over the earth.
8. Israel will dwell securely in peace.

Next: "In the Name of Jesus"

CHAPTER 17

In the Name of Jesus

Jesus ministered to the Jewish people for a little over three years. We say this because there are three Passovers recorded in the gospel of John, and Jesus was crucified on the third one. In his first year of ministry, Jesus taught his followers to pray to his Father (Matt. 6:9). Then, as his ministry was drawing to a close, he made these statements:

> Hitherto (up to now), you have asked nothing in my name; ask and you shall receive. (John 16:24)

> Whatever you shall ask the Father in my name, he will give it to you. (John 16:23)

> If you reside in me, and my words reside in you, whatever you determine, ask, and it will come into being. (John 15:7)

> Truly, truly, I (Jesus) say to you, he that believes into me, the works that I do shall he do

also; and greater works than these shall he do because I go to my Father. Whatever you ask in my name, <u>that will I do</u>, that the Father may be glorified in the Son. If you ask anything in my name, <u>I will do it</u>. (John 14:12–14)

Question: What has changed that allows the believer to ask and pray in the name of Jesus?

The simple answer, as he tells us, is that he (Jesus) is going back to the Father (John 16:16), going back to where he was before (John 16:28; John 17:4–5) and returning there as a glorified man (John 13:31–32). While ministering on earth to his generation, Jesus told us (1) that he can do nothing of himself (i.e., he laid down his God nature in order to become a man) (Phil. 2:6–7) but that he does that which he sees his Father doing (John 5:19) and (2) that his teaching is not his but that of his Father (John 7:16). As Christians, we recognize that Jesus and his disciples were ministering in the power of the Holy Spirit (John 14:17; Gal. 5:25). "The works that I (Jesus) do," said Jesus, "you shall do also, and greater works because I go to the Father" (John 14:12). "If you ask anything in my name, <u>I will do it</u>." What has changed is his position! Before the incarnation, Jesus was the Lord of hosts, but he laid aside the powers and authority associated with that position and became the man Jesus Christ. Through the cross (John 10:17–18), Jesus knew that he was going home and that he would again share in that relationship that he had with his Father before his birth in Bethlehem (John 17:5). There are two things that appear interesting in the kenosis relationship established when the Father sent his Son:

a) John 3:13 indicates that even while Jesus was visibly ministering on earth that he was still present in heaven.

b) John 10:17–18 tells us that Jesus had the authority to lay down his life and to pick it up again. These two verses tell me three things: (1) Jesus had the authority to scuttle his mission and resume his initial position with the Father with no questions asked. (2) The nails did not fix him to the cross (Matt. 27:39–40). He could have come off the cross and destroyed the whole earth (Matt. 26:53). (3) They give some insight to Ephesians 2:6, which reads: "He (the Father) raised us up together, and made us sit together in heavenly places in Christ Jesus."

Acts chapter 3 and 4 tell us there is power in the name of Jesus (Acts 3:16, 4:12).

The event recorded in Acts chapters 3 and 4 occurred in the temple at Jerusalem shortly after the Holy Spirit was poured out upon the church (i.e., on the first Pentecost after the crucifixion). As Peter and John were going to the temple for prayer, they healed a crippled man, saying, "In the name of Jesus Christ of Nazareth, rise up and walk" (Acts 3:6). The Jewish authorities, who had opposed Jesus and had him executed, arrested Peter and John, demanding to know what happened.

"By what power or by what name have you done this miracle?" they asked.

"We did this in the name of Jesus Christ of Nazareth," they replied (Acts 4:7–10).

And so, the high priest commanded them not to speak at all nor teach in the name of Jesus (Acts 4:18). The book of Acts is full of miracles, signs, and wonders performed in the name of Jesus. The early Christian church was threatened, persecuted, and legally harassed, but the name of Jesus was spread throughout the known world. The effect of the early church on the world of its day is perhaps best captured in Acts 17:6 when the citizens of Thessalonica protested to their rulers at the coming of the apostle Paul's ministry, saying, "These are they that have turned the world upside down, and now they have come here too."

And so it is written "that at the name of Jesus every knee should bow in heaven, and in earth, and under the earth: And every tongue confess that Jesus Christ is Lord, to the glory of God the Father" **(Phil. 2:10–11).**

And so we believe.

> And these signs shall follow them that believe; <u>in the name of Jesus</u> they shall cast out demons; they shall speak with new tongues… They shall lay hands on the sick, and the sick shall recover. **(Mark 16:17–18)**

Next: "Chapter Summaries by Key Verses"

CHAPTER 18

Chapter Summaries by Key Verses

Chapter 1: Malachi 3:1

I (Lord of hosts) will send John the Baptist (Matt. 11:9–11) before my face: and the Adon (Jesus Christ) (Ps. 110:1; Matt. 22:42–45) whom you seek will come to his temple. **(Mal. 3:1)**

Chapter 2: Revelation 1:1

The revelation (*apokalupsis*) of Jesus Christ, which God (the Father) gave to him, to show his servants. **(Rev. 1:1)**

I (Jesus) am the first and the last: I am he that lives, and was dead, and, behold, I am alive for evermore. **(Rev. 1:17–18)**

Chapter 3: Who Are You?

Even the same that I said unto you <u>from the beginning</u>. **(John 8:25)**

Hearken unto me (the Lord of Hosts), O Jacob and Israel, my called; <u>I am he; I am the first, I also am the last</u>. My hand has laid the foundation of the earth, and the palm of my right hand has spread out the heavens: When I call unto them, they stand up together... Come near to me, and hear this; I have not spoken in secret <u>from the beginning</u>; from the time that it was, there am I: And now the Lord God, and his Spirit has sent me. **(Isa. 48:12–16)**

Chapter 4: The Word of God

The word of the Lord (Yehovah) came to Abram in a vision, saying, Fear not, Abram: I am thy shield, and your exceeding great reward. **(Gen. 15:1)**

In the beginning was the Word (Jesus), and he was with God, and he was God. He was in the beginning with God. All things were made through him; and without him was not anything made that was made. **(John 1:1–3)**

For there are three that bear record in heaven, the Father, the Word, and the Holy Spirit: and these three are one. **(1 John 5:7)**

Chapter 5: The Kenosis

For although he (Jesus) was in the form (3444 *morphe*) of God...he emptied (2758 *kenoo*) himself, taking on the form (3444) of a slave, becoming in the likeness of men: And in fashion being found as a man, he humbled himself, and became obedient unto death, even the death of the cross. **(Phil. 2:6–8)**

And the Word became flesh and lived among us. **(John 1:14)**

Chapter 6: I Am in the Father, and the Father Is in Me

That God (the Father) was in Christ, reconciling the world to himself. **(2 Cor. 5:19)**

Do you not believe that I am in the Father, and the Father in me? The words that I speak to you I speak not of myself; but the Father that dwells in me, he does the works. **(John 14:10)**

The only begotten Son, who is in the bosom of the Father, he reveals him. **(John 1:18)**

Chapter 7: The Messiah

To his disciples Jesus asked, "Who do the people say that I am?" They replied, "Some say you are Elijah, or Jeremiah, or one of the other prophets." Then Jesus asked them, "But who do you say that I am." <u>You are the Christ (the Messiah), the Son of the living God</u>, replied Simon Peter. Jesus responded, "Flesh and blood has not revealed this to you, but my Father which is in heaven, and <u>it is upon this rock that I will build my church</u>, and the gates of hades shall not prevail against it." (**Matt. 16:13–18**)

Chapter 8: The Suffering Messiah

He was oppressed and afflicted, yet he opened not his mouth: He is brought as a lamb to the slaughter, and as a sheep before her shearers is dumb, so he opened not his mouth, He was taken from prison and from judgment… For he was cut off out of the land of the living: For the transgression of my people was he stricken. (**Isa. 53:7–8**)

And the eunuch asked Philip, "Who does the prophet speak of?" And then Philip began at that scripture (Isa. 53:7–8; Acts 8:32–33) and preached unto him Jesus. (**Acts 8:34–35**)

Chapter 9: The King of Israel

Rejoice greatly, O daughter of Zion; shout, O daughter of Jerusalem: Behold, <u>your King</u> comes unto you: He is just, and having salvation; lowly, and riding upon an ass, and upon a colt the foal of an ass. (**Zech. 9:9**)

And Pilate set over Jesus' head a plaque saying, THIS IS JESUS THE KING OF THE JEWS. (**Matt. 27:37**)

I have set my king upon my holy hill of Zion," saith the Lord. (**Ps. 2:6**)

Chapter 10: Moses Wrote of Me

For had you believed Moses, you would have believed me: for he wrote of me. **(John 5:46)**

And God (430—*Elohiym*) spoke to Moses saying, "I am the Lord (Yehovah): I appeared to Abraham, Issac, and Jacob as El Shadday (God Almighty), but by my name Yehovah (the Lord) I was not known to them." **(Exod. 6:3)**

And they (those who have overcome the antichrist) sing the song of Moses the servant of God and the song of the Lamb saying, "Great and marvellous are your works, <u>Lord God Almighty</u>; just and true are your ways, thou King of saints, who shall not fear thee." **(Rev. 15:3)**

Then sang Moses and the children of Israel this song unto the Lord saying, "The Lord is a man of war: Yehovah is his name." **(Exod. 15:1–3)**

Chapter 11: The Lamb of God

Regarding Jesus, John the Baptist said, "Behold the Lamb of God, which takes away the sin of the world." **(John 1:29)**

And they (the church) overcame him (Satan) by the blood of the Lamb, and by the word of their testimony, and they loved not their lives even unto death. **(Rev. 12:11)**

Chapter 12: Coming and Going

I came forth (1831—issued forth) from the Father, and came into the world: again, I leave the world, and go to the Father. **(John 16:28)**

And now, O Father, glorify me with your own self with the glory which I had with you before the world was. (Mic. 5:2–4; **John 17:5)**

Chapter 13: I Will Return to My Place

I will go and return to my place, till they acknowledge their offence, and seek my face: In their affliction they will seek me early. **(Hosea 5:15)**

You (Jerusalem) shall not see me again, till you say, "Blessed is he that comes in the name of the Lord." **(Matt. 23:39;** Ps. 118:26)

The Lord (Yehovah) said to my Lord (Adon), sit at my right hand, until I make your enemies your footstool. **(Ps. 110:1)**

I (Jesus) will come again, and receive you to myself, that where I am, there you may be also. **(John 14:3)**

Chapter 14: The Wrath of God

Why do the Gentiles rage, and the community of God imagine a vain thing? The kings of the earth set themselves, and the rulers take counsel together against the Lord and his Messiah saying, "Let us break their bands asunder, and cast away their cords from us." He that sits in the heavens shall laugh, the Lord shall have them in derision: He shall speak unto them in his wrath, and vex them in his sore displeasure. **(Ps. 2:1–5)**

The nations were angry, and <u>your wrath has come</u>...and the time is come to destroy those which corrupt the earth. **(Rev. 11:18)**

And they (the kings of the earth, the great men of the earth) said to the mountains and rocks, "Fall on us, and hide us from the face of him that sits on the throne, and from <u>the wrath of the Lamb</u>: For the great day of his wrath is come, and who shall be able to stand?" **(Rev. 6:15–17;** Ps. 2:12)

Chapter 15: The Day of the Lord

Whom did you dread and fear, so that you lied, and did not remember me, did not even give me a thought. Have I not held my peace, even for a long time, and so you do not fear me? **(Isa. 57:11)**

These things you have done and I have been silent; you thought that I was one like yourself, but now I rebuke you, and lay the charge before you. **(Ps. 50:21)**

This is the day whereof I have spoken, says the Lord God. **(Ezek. 39:8)**

And when the seventh angel poured out his vial of wrath into the air; there came a voice out of the temple of heaven, from the throne, saying, "It is done." **(Rev. 16:17)**

Chapter 16: Thy Kingdom Come

And he shall stand and feed in the strength of Yehovah, in the majesty of the name of the Lord his God; and they (Israel) shall abide: For now he shall be great unto the ends of the earth. **(Mic. 5:4)**

The Lord (Yehovah) has taken away your judgments, he has cast out your enemies: The King of Israel, even the Lord (Yehovah) is in your midst: you shall not see evil any more. **(Zeph. 3:15)**

And the time came that the saints (Jude 3; Rom. 1:7; Eph. 4:12) possessed the kingdom. **(Dan. 7:22)**

In the regeneration (3824—the new beginning, the reconstitution) when the Son of man sits in the throne of his glory (Mark 14:62), you shall sit upon twelve thrones judging the twelve tribes of Israel. **(Matt. 19:28)**

And they (saints) shall reign with him (Jesus) a thousand years. **(Rev. 20:6)**

Chapter 17: In the Name of Jesus

Truly, truly, I (Jesus) say to you, he that believes into me, the works that I do shall he do also; and greater works than these shall he do because I go to my Father. Whatever you ask in my name, <u>that will I do</u>, that the Father may be glorified in the Son. If you ask anything in my name, <u>I will do it</u>. **(John 14:12–14)**

Next: "Who Is Jesus: The Summary Statement"

CHAPTER 19

Who Is Jesus: The Summary Statement

Here is what we've come to know:

1. Jesus was in the beginning with God the Father (John 1:1; Isa. 48:16; John 17:5).
2. All things were created through Jesus and for Jesus (Col. 1:16; Rev. 4:11; John 1:3).
3. Jesus is the image of the invisible God (Col. 1:15; Heb. 1:3).
4. Jesus reveals/explains God the Father (John 1:18).
5. Nothing comes to the Father except through Jesus (John 14:6).
6. If you know Jesus, you know the Father (John 14:7–9).
7. Jesus and the Father are one (John 10:30; Deut. 6:4).
8. The Father is greater (bigger) than Jesus (John 14:28; John 10:29).

9. Jesus is in the Father, and the Father is in him (John 14:10–11).
10. Jesus emptied out himself (laid aside his God attributes) to become a man (Phil. 2:6–8; Gal. 4:4; John 1:14).
11. Jesus is the Son of Man (Phil. 2:6–8; Mark 14:62; Matt. 24:30).
12. Jesus is God in the flesh (John 1:14; Matt. 1:23; Isa. 7:14).
13. Jesus today sits in the right hand of God (Ps. 110:1; Heb. 1:3).
14. Jesus exists today in a glorified human body (John 20:19 and 26; Phil. 3:21; Rom. 8:23; 1 Cor. 15:53).
15. Jesus is the firstborn of every formation (Col. 1:15; Rev. 3:14; 1 Cor. 15:23).
16. Jesus is building a spiritual temple (Zech. 6:12–13; Eph. 2:21–22).
17. Jesus is coming again (John 14:3; 2 Thess. 2:1; Titus 2:13; Rev. 19:11–16; Acts 1:11; Zech. 14:1–5).
18. Jesus will reign over the whole earth (Rev. 20:4–6; Isa. 2:2–4; Mic. 5:4).
19. And of his kingdom, there is no end (Dan. 7:14; Rev. 22:1–5).

Therefore, using the above scriptures, we make the following statement:

In the beginning God (*Elohiym*) created the heavens and the earth (Gen. 1:1). *Elohiym*, the word used for God in Genesis 1:1, is a singular plural noun indicating that while God is one that he is more than one. Jesus was in the beginning <u>with</u> God (the Father) (John 1:1). In John 1:1, the Greek word *pros* is being translated as our English word <u>*with*</u>, but the word *pros* literally means that Jesus was by the side of God the Father when he created the heavens and the earth. All things were created (came into being) through Jesus, and without him, nothing came into being (John 1:3; Col. 1:16; Rev. 4:11). Jesus is the image of the invisible Father (Colossians 1:15; Hebrews 1:2). No one (nothing) can look upon the Father (John 1:18; Exod. 33:20; 1 Tim. 6:16).

The Father reveals himself to his creation only through his Son (John 1:18), and Jesus is the only way to know the Father (John 14:7–9; John 1:18). When the time was right, Jesus laid down his godly attributes and became a man (Gal. 4:4; Phil. 2:6–8). This does not mean that he ceased to be God (John 3:13), for while he walked the earth, he was God in the flesh (John 1:14; Isa. 7:14; Matt. 1:23; 2 Cor. 5:19). God the Father was in him, and he was in the Father (John 14:10), and the works (miracles) that he did bore witness to this relationship (John 14:11). And we (the children of Adam) killed the author of life (Acts 3:15), but this was in accordance with God's plan for mankind from the beginning of the world (Acts 2:23; Eph. 3:9). It is for this reason that Jesus is known as the one who is and was and is to come (Rev. 4:8–11; Rev. 11:17–18).

He is the one who has triumphed over the grave, and he is now alive forever more (Rev. 1:17–18). Before he took on the nature of a man, he <u>was</u> known as the Angel of the Lord (Exod. 3:2–8), the Lord of hosts (Isa. 44:6), and the Lord God Almighty (Exod. 6:2–3). After his resurrection from the dead, Jesus returned to his rightful place in heaven, and he currently sits in the right hand of God the Father (Ps. 110:1; Heb. 1:3). And he <u>is to come</u> again for his church (John 14:2–3). Scripture tells us that there is a day coming when Jesus will return for his church (2 Thess. 2:1). This event is commonly known as the rapture of the church (Luke 17:34–37; 1 Thess. 4:14–17). It is the day in which those who are spiritually in Christ (both living and dead) will receive a glorified body, just like Jesus's resurrected body (Rom. 8:23; 1 Cori. 15:50–53). The day of rapture is a parousia, a coming near. Jesus will come in the sky for his church and take it to heaven (Matthew 24:30–31), shortly after Jesus will return physically to earth with his glorified saints to destroy his enemies and adversaries (Zech. 14:1–5; Rev. 19:11–21; Ps. 110:5–6, and establish his millennial kingdom (Dan. 7:7–18; Rev. 20:4–6).

Today, Jesus, the branch of David, is building the temple of the Lord (Zech. 6:12–13). It is not a brick-and-mortar building but a spiritual temple made up of living stones (1 Pet. 2:5), a dwelling place for God in the Spirit (Eph. 2:21–22). This spiritual temple is also known as the bride of Christ (Rev. 19:7; Rev. 21:1–2) and/or the church of God (Eph. 1:22–23; Matthew 16:18). In the book of Revelation, we see the bride of Christ residing in the new heaven and new earth in the city of New Jerusalem (Rev. 21:1–2). In the new heaven and new earth, the dwelling place of God is with men (Rev. 21:3), for the glory, which God the Father gave to the Son of Man, will he also give to his church (John 17:22; Col. 3:4; 1 John 3:2; Phil. 3:21). As the book of Revelation draws to a close, we see the Lord God Almighty and the Lamb abiding together in the city of New Jerusalem as one, for they are inseparable (Rev. 21:22–23; Rev. 22:3).

Next: "Knowing Jesus"

CHAPTER 20

Knowing Jesus

The plight of the five foolish virgins.

The bridegroom came; and those who were ready went with him to the marriage (Rev. 19:7), and the door was shut.

Afterward came the five foolish virgins, saying, "Lord, Lord, open to us."

But the Lord answered them saying, "I know you not."

—Matt. 25:10–12

If you want to be on the right side of history, it's very important that you know Jesus. It's important because God has purposed (Eph. 3:11) and planned to place all things in heaven and earth under his Son, Jesus Christ (Eph. 1:10). Jesus said, "If you are not with me, you are against me; and whoever is against me shall be scattered" (Matt. 12:30). God the Father, through his Son, desires to have a living relationship with you (Matt. 25:10–12), and he has sent Jesus to atone for your sins, and he has sent the Holy Spirit to give you the ability to live a holy life. In the end, it will not matter what men think or say but what God has determined. Jesus said, "I am the resurrection and the life: he that believes in me, though he were dead, yet shall he live: and whosoever lives and believes in me shall never die" (John 10:25–26). It is written that in the end, everyone will confess that Jesus is Lord to the glory of God the Father. However, the distinction is this: If today we voluntarily choose to make Jesus Christ our Lord, there is salvation (safety) in his name. But if we balk or rebel against him, there is only judgment that awaits us. No man can afford to reject this offer from God, for it is not the Father's will that any man should perish but that all should come to a saving faith in Christ Jesus. The bottom line is this: Don't be on the wrong side of history, and don't be caught dead without Jesus.

Jesus once told a parable about a merchant who dealt in pearls, until a day when he found a pearl of great price, and then he sold all that he had and bought it (Matt. 13:45–46). Jesus is that pearl of great price. Think about it! We spend our lives in commerce. We pursue the American dream. We buy homes and real estate, but there is no real permanency in them. Any number of things, such as poor national leadership, wars, economic upsets, and death, can and do take our future away. In this world, one thing is certain: Naked we came into this world, and naked we shall leave it. Only Jesus Christ gives us the hope of a certain sustained future full of peace and security, and only Jesus can give us the victory over the grave (1 Cor. 15:21–22; Rev. 1:17–18).

The apostle Paul, while on his way to Damascus, found the pearl of great price. Here is what he did (Phil. 3:7–9): He changed the priorities of his life. He gave up those things that he had previously considered to be paramount, and he was willing to lose everything that he had gained in his life in order to be <u>found in Christ</u>. Jesus said, "If a man loves me, he will keep (5083—to guard, to watch over) my words: and my Father will love him, and we will come unto him, and make our abode with him" (John 14:23).

You may ask, "How can God come and make his home with the believer?" The answer involves the Holy Spirit, which is the spirit of Christ (Gal. 4:6), and the Holy Spirit resides in the believer (1 Cor. 6:19; Col. 1:27). The work of the Holy Spirit is to make the believer like Christ (Rom. 8:29), and the believer's work is to allow the Holy Spirit to complete his assigned task.

Perhaps, through these chapters, you too have found the pearl of great price, and you are asking yourself, "What can I do to buy this pearl?" The foremost key is to believe (Rom. 10:9–10). If you confess with your mouth the Lord Jesus Christ and believe in your heart that God raised him from the dead, you shall be saved (made safe). For with the heart, man believes into righteousness, and with the mouth, confession is made into salvation.

Next, you should pray this prayer or a similar prayer: "Father, I believe that Jesus died for my sins and that you raised him from the dead. I acknowledge my sins and past failures, and I acknowledge that I need the Holy Spirit in my life. And I am asking that the spirit of Jesus come into my heart and make me like him. These things I ask and pray for in the precious name of Jesus. Amen."

If you have prayed and are serious about your new life in Christ, do these three things: (1) Tell someone that you just asked Jesus into your heart. (2) Get involved in a gospel-believing church. And (3) start studying the Bible by first reading through the Gospel of John.

Last but not least, remember this: If any man is in Christ, he is a new creation. The old things have passed away—all things are new (2 Cor. 5:17). Now, my prayer for you is that the Father of our Lord Jesus Christ, the Father of glory, strengthens you with his might in your inner man through the Holy Spirit of promise that has been given to us in Jesus's name. Amen.

Go in peace (April 3, 2024). Grow in Christ. The Lord comes.

About the Author

Who is he? He is a young seventy-seven-year-old man. He has three children, three grandchildren, and one great-grandchild. He asked Jesus into his heart in 1963, and in June 1965, he entered the US Navy. In 1971, thanks to the GI Bill, he attended Murray State University. In 1973, during the Charismatic Renewal, he rededicated his life to our Lord Jesus Christ, and he has been walking with him ever since. He spent most of his life working in the nuclear power industry. During his working years, he attended and served as an elder and deacon in several churches in South Jersey. Since retiring in 2005, he has written three Christian books for the Lord. The first, *Something to Think About: Things Not Taught in School*, discusses the tenets of our Christian faith. The second, *Come and See*, builds a case favoring a post-trib rapture. And now, this third book, *Knowing Jesus: Being on the Right Side of History*, speaks of Jesus as he who is and was and is to come and tells of his soon coming kingdom.

www.ingramcontent.com/pod-product-compliance
Lightning Source LLC
Chambersburg PA
CBHW031427130726
47989CB00003B/1052